How to Talk To

KIDS

About Bullying

Parents & teachers guide with effective strategies on how to identify & deal with social & school bullying, cyberbullying and stop Teens bullies

ROB HECTOR

Text Copyright © Rob Hector

All rights reserved. No part of this guide may be reproduced in any form without permission in writing from the publisher except in the case of brief quotations embodied in critical articles or reviews.

Legal & Disclaimer

The information contained in this book and its contents is not designed to replace or take the place of any form of medical or professional advice; and is not meant to replace the need for independent medical, financial, legal or other professional advice or services, as may be required. The content and information in this book has been provided for educational and entertainment purposes only.

The content and information contained in this book has been compiled from sources deemed reliable, and it is accurate to the best of the Author's knowledge, information and belief. However, the Author cannot guarantee its accuracy and validity and cannot be held liable for any errors and/or omissions. Further, changes are periodically made to this book as and when needed. Where appropriate and/or necessary, you must consult a professional (including but not limited to your doctor, attorney, financial advisor or such other professional advisor) before using any of the suggested remedies, techniques, or information in this book.

Upon using the contents and information contained in this book, you agree to hold harmless the Author from and against any damages, costs, and expenses, including any legal fees potentially resulting from the application of any of the information provided by this book. This disclaimer applies to any loss, damages or injury caused by the use and application, whether directly or indirectly, of any advice or information presented, whether for breach of contract, tort, negligence, personal injury, criminal intent, or under any other cause of action.

You agree to accept all risks of using the information presented inside this book.

You agree that by continuing to read this book, where appropriate and/or necessary, you shall consult a professional (including but not limited to your doctor, attorney, or financial advisor or such other advisor as needed) before using any of the suggested remedies, techniques, or information in this book.

TABLE OF CONTENTS

Introduction 1

Chapter 1: Defining School Bullying And Its Many Forms 11

Chapter 2: Identifying the Signs of Bullying 19

Chapter 3: The Effects of Bullying 24

Chapter 4: Myths about bullying............................ 30

Chapter 5: Bullying Misconceptions...................... 36

    Only Boys are Bullies 37

    Bully will go away if avoided/ignored................. 37

    Being Bullied Builds Character 38

    Handle Bullying on Their Own........................... 38

    Bully is Just an Attention Seeker 39

    Vulnerability: Who is at Risk?............................ 39

Chapter 6: Understanding bullies........................... 45

Chapter 7: Child prevention 52

Chapter 8: Finding Support from People Around . 72

Chapter 9: Why do teenagers bully? 79

Who Gets Bullied? What is wrong with them? .. 81

How to Spot Bullying?... 83

Chapter 10: Victim on the bully.............................. 87

Chapter 11: A Necessity For Teenagers To Avoid Being Bullied 99

Encouraging Good Behavior in Teenagers 102

Who Needs to Act and who is acting for its Prevention? 105

Concrete actions/tips to avoid Physical, Verbal, Social, Psychological and Cyber Bullying.......... 111

For Students: 111

For Teachers.. 112

Parents... 112

Chapter 12: What To Do When You Spot A Bully? 114

Don't Join or Watch... 115

Stop Rumors.. 115

Stay Firm and Offer Support............................. 116

Tell an Adult 116

Spare No Details 116

Seek Support 117

Encourage Reporting Bullying 117

    Listen Without Judgement 118

    Educate 119

Chapter 13: Bullying and Suicide - Does it Make Sense? 120

    Cyberbullying 121

    Growing Up Online – How do they bully you? 124

    Harmful Effects of Cyberbullying 127

Chapter 14: Dealing with Cyberbullying 130

Chapter 15: Other Things That Should Be Remembered About Cyberbullying 135

Chapter 16: Benefits of Bullying 140

Chapter 17: The Bullying Epidemic 146

Conclusion 150

Introduction

This book is all about bullies. It tells what a bully is, how they act. It tells you what to do if you are being bullied. It tells you how to know if someone else is being bullied. You will learn how a bully looks like and how they act. You will learn what to do if a bully comes to you and is mean. You will learn the different types of bullies. By learning how to recognize a bully you can learn how to react if one comes to you or one of your friends.

What Is a Bully?

A bully is a mean person. A bully is a strong person. A bully is mean to people smaller than they are. A bully sometimes likes to push someone who is shorter than they are. A bully will be cruel to people who are not as strong as they are. To be cruel means to be mean. A bully may call people bad names. A bully may take things from others by force. A bully may shove people.

Does a Bully Show Good Behavior?

A bully act badly. Bad behavior is what a bully has. Good behavior means being nice. Bullies are not nice. Good behavior means not calling people names. Bullies like to speak badly toward others. Good behavior means people will help others. Bullies do not help others. Good behavior means the strong people help the weak. Bullies will hurt the weak.

What Does a Bully Look Like?

You will recognize a bully when you see they are strong but are being mean to those who are weak. Bullies may have a frown on their face. Bullies may shove someone for no good reason. Bullies will talk badly about others. Bullies will not help someone who is in need. Bullies will laugh at someone who is hurt.

What Does a Bullied Person Look Like?

The person who is being bullied may look like you or me. They are nice and have done nothing wrong. They may be scared. They may want to run and hide when they see the bully.

Why Does a Bully Act the Way They Do?

Bullies may want attention so they act badly towards others to get it. Bullies may feel that by acting bad they are popular with some people. Bullies act bad to get their way, what they want. Bullies like to feel powerful. Bullies may be this way because their family is always shouting and mad. Bullies might act badly because they think it is normal. Bullies may be bad because they are copying another bully. Bullies may not know how much they hurt others. They may think acting bad is okay. Bullies may not care what others think. A bully may be someone who is being bullied by someone bigger and more powerful than him or her.

Different Kinds of Bullying

Attention seeking bullies will do something mean to you when are around to see it. They may speak badly or hurtful. They may make fun of you because others are watching. They think it is funny.

Cyber bullies will use the internet and cell phones to send mean messages. They may leave mean comments or threats on to you on your phone. They may send mean messages on your social media accounts.

Excluding bullies are people who will leave you out of a group just out of meanness. They may also talk bad about you in front of others making you feel badly.

Intimidating bullies like to scare you into doing what they want. They may intimidate you into being mean to another person. They may frighten you into doing something that is against the rules.

Physical bullies are people who like to start fights. They may hit, punch, or shove another person. They may steal things and destroy it.

Rumor spreading bullies will spread lies about people. They like to talk about others, spreading stories about them that are not true. They like to make trouble for others behind their backs.

Verbal bullies like to use their mouth to hurt others. They may call you names. They may poke fun of something different about you. They may make fun of your skin color, your weight, your height, the color of your clothes. They like to use words to make people hurt.

Effects of Bullying

Bullying affects both the person who is doing the bullying and the person who is being bullied.

For the person being bullied they may feel down about it. They may be anxious. They may feel alone. They may feel hopeless. They may feel sick even. Their school grades may go down. They may want to drop out of school.

For the bully the effects may turn into abuse later. They may start to drink alcohol or take drugs. They may get into many fights. They may drop out of school. They may get into trouble with the law. They may be a bully when they grow up to their own family.

What to Do If Someone Bullies You

If a bully comes after you try to ignore them. Sometimes if you ignore them, they will stop. Ignore the bully by not looking at them. Ignore them by turning away from them and acting as if they are not there. If they do not stop, you should pretend the bully is doing something funny. Sometimes when you imagine something funny, you will not be as scared. A bully may only do these things to scare you. If you show them you are not scared, they may stop. Try to think of good things and be around others who are nice to you. Do not show the bully you are scared, even if you are. Try to talk nicely to the bully. If that does not work and the bully still bothers you ask someone for help when the bully comes around. Ask your friends to help you. Ask your teachers to help you.

What to Do If Someone Else is Being Bullied and You See It

If you see someone being bullied first talk to them about it. Tell them you care about them. Try to help them by being their friend. Invite them to be friends with your friends. Tell the bully to leave them alone. If the bully keeps being mean to them or to you, tell someone else about it. Tell other friends about the bully. Tell your teachers about the bully. Tell any adults in your school about the bully. It is okay to tell the counselor or the principal.

How to Stop Bullying

Talk about bullying with your parents, friends, and teachers. Encourage them to talk about it if they are being bullied. Ask for help in dealing with a bully. Offer to help someone who is being bullied. Talk to the bully about stopping. Ask an adult to talk to the bully. You behave. You give the bully a good example to follow if you are behaving.

How Can Your Parents Help If You Are Bullied?

Parents can help you by first talking with your teachers in school if you are being bullied. Parents can teach you how to react when a bully starts to be mean to you. Parents can teach you how to walk away. Parents can teach you how to go to your friends. Parents can teach you how to talk to the bully. Parents can help you have confidence to face the bully. Parents should discourage fighting. Parents should teach you how to defend yourself. If a bully is hitting you, parents should teach you how to run to another adult for help. If there is no other adult around, ask your parents what you should do if the bully is physically mean and you cannot run.

Apart from the inevitable horrors of puberty, there's one thing that both parents and children fear and it has nothing to do with monsters lurking in the closet (imaginary or otherwise).

It's something that most people experience at some point in their lives, as well as something that one can't quite forget.

Bullying is so common in schools all around the world that most movies set during a person's school years usually feature an archetypical bully as one of the characters. The actual statistics behind this occurrence is no laughing matter, however.

The American Psychological Association, for instance, estimates that the percentage of schoolchildren who experience one or more forms of bullying throughout their school careers range from 40 - 80 %, and that while children who come from lower socio-economic backgrounds have a higher tendency to be bullied, those who come from more affluent families don't do that much better.

In Canada, about 1 in 3 students often report being the target or victim of specific forms of bullying, while 47% of parents have complained that their children were bullied at school.

The advent of the Internet and social media has also resulted in a more pervasive form of bullying that persists even after the victim has left the school premises. Cyber-bullying, which is a form of bullying that is enacted online, has been experienced by about 73% of bullying victims.

This particular form of bullying takes many forms, all of which range from the sending of aggressive, threatening emails or private messages to the target, the sharing of photos or other private content that often expose the target to a great deal of shame and humiliation, and even the consistent and targeted smear campaigns carried out on any and all forms of social media.

What makes these statistics far more disturbing is that experts have estimated the actual number of bullying victims to be significantly higher, as approximately 60% of bullying victims often don't come forward.

Also, while the most obvious victim would appear to be the target, bullying also has a far-reaching negative impact on the bully and the school community. Thus, it's hardly surprising that a lot of schools have taken a hard-line position and adopted a zero-tolerance approach to bullying on their campuses.

However, despite plenty of schools taking the said position, it's natural that many parents are still concerned about how their kids will fare in the sometimes-dog-eat-dog world of adolescent education.

How does one ever understand the process and the reasons behind bullying?

What can a parent do to ensure that their child can stand up for himself or herself in the event of a bullying episode?

And should a child be the victim of an unfortunate incident, what should a parent do to minimize the damage to their kid's development?

Lastly, how should a parent react upon finding out that their own child is the one bullying others?

The next few chapters of this book will attempt to delve into the answers to the key questions mentioned above.

Chapter One

DEFINING SCHOOL BULLYING AND ITS MANY FORMS

Bullying is any act where someone in a position of power uses his or her natural advantage to coerce someone weaker into doing something against the latter's will. It can also involve using force or intimidation into shaming or injuring another person in more ways than one.

Bullying can take place at home, in the office, in the outside world, but perhaps the most common venue for it is at school.

School bullying takes place in any educational institution, and can manifest itself in verbal, physical, or even sexual abuse. In some cases, incidents of school bullying have involved all three of the said forms.

While bullying can take many different forms, it

is usually characterized by the presence of certain factors, namely:

1) The conscious intent to inflict harm and/or humiliation upon one person or a specific group of persons. Bullies do not hurt other people by accident; they do so with an undeniable intent. Also, most bullies pick their victims according to a certain criteria, be it the victim's race, size, gender, and so on.

2) Repetitive incidents. Bullying incidents are hardly ever one-time affairs. Since bullies select their victims carefully, they tend to subject them to a constant and sustained barrage of spiteful behavior.

3) An inequity of power. A lot of bullies tend to have the advantage when it comes to physical strength, beauty, charisma, popularity, or even socio-economic standing. Thus, they seek out individuals who are notably lacking in such things to better lord it over their targeted victims. It should be noted, however, that sometimes a bully needs only a perceived imbalance of power and not necessarily an actual

advantage as the impetus to bully someone. Hence, incidents of bullying can also occur between two people who are more or less equal in stature.

4) Progressive aggression. Apart from being repetitive, bullying can also escalate as the bully gets some sort of high from inflicting harm upon his victims. Often, many victims have experienced being the recipient of spiteful emails one day, and then being on the receiving end of an actual physical blow the next.

5) Trauma or distress. The target of a bullying incident experiences varying degrees of physical, social, or psychological trauma. Some victims suffer mild to moderate scratches and/or bruising, while some may end up withdrawn and with a marked reluctance to engage with anyone at school.

There are basically two kinds of bullying. Direct bullying involves an outright attack on a target that usually involves a physical and verbal attack.

This kind of bullying also often takes place in the

open, and can be characterized by at least one of the following forms:

1) Physical bullying. This is perhaps the most common kind of bullying, and is the easiest to detect. It involves any kind of unwelcome physical contact from a victim's aggressor, and may often involve the use of force or violence. Pushing, shoving, kicking all count as forms of physical bullying, but so too can seemingly milder gestures like tickling and pinching. Inappropriate or unwelcome touching also counts as physical bullying.

2) Verbal bullying. This entails the use of foul or derogatory language to besmirch a person's name or reputation or to belittle their self-esteem. The constant harassment of another person by negatively commenting on their looks, clothes, or form and/or engaging in below-the-belt teasing is also classified as a form of verbal bullying.

3) Sexual bullying. While the term might imply practices like groping or the

coercion of young girls into performing sexual favors, sexual bullying actually encompasses any malicious act that uses a person's sexuality against them. Boys and girls can both be victims of such, but adolescent females are the most common victims and are usually subjected to insulting language that demeans their gender either to their face, behind their back, or on a social media platform.

4) Pack bullying. This involves a crowd of people ganging up on one or a few individuals. Pack bullies can use physical force, slanderous language, or a combination of both. This practice is more common in public high schools, where the presence of inner-city gangs can rile up passersby to take part.

5) Emotional bullying. This inflicts mild to severe damage upon the victim's self-esteem or psyche, and can range from the willful isolation of certain individual from groups to the spreading of false and utterly nasty rumors about individuals or groups.

Indirect bullying, on the other hand, is far more subtle but is arguably the more insidious of the two.

Since it often takes place behind a victim's back in the form of underhanded tactics such as rumor-spreading, backstabbing, manipulation, and social isolation, it is harder to detect and its effects can be far more damaging.

Cyber bullying is one form of indirect bullying, as a child or an adolescent can use an anonymous identity to torment his or her peers or classmates by way of the Internet or through the use of mobile smart phones and other similar gadgets.

And while anyone (regardless of their grade level, social status, physical build, or intellectual capacity) can be a victim of bullying, school bullies often target individuals or groups who belong to one or more of the following categories:

1) Students dealing with gender or sexual orientation issues. Heterosexual adolescents can sometimes bully their homosexual or bisexual peers for being different from them or to take out their

own sexual identity frustration. Homophobic beliefs and/or behaviors, which are sometimes knowingly or unknowingly reinforced at the bully's home, can also contribute to this.

2) Students who belong to the minority race. Just as children of color can be bullied by white kids at a school with a predominantly Caucasian population, so too can white kids be bullied by students who belong to the prevailing race at school. Xenophobia, or the irrational fear towards foreigners, be it latent or active, is oftentimes to blame.

3) Students with specific religious beliefs. Certain religions, such as Islam, require its followers to dress or behave in a particular way (such as wearing an hijab, abstaining from pork, or engaging in prayer at certain times of the day). Students who belong to such religions often become the targets of bullying simply for being different from their peers.

4) Students who suffer from physical disabilities or deformities. Since

adolescence is often a time where physical appearance and robustness becomes paramount, teenagers who are physically handicapped or somehow deformed are often made to be the butt of jokes among their peers.

Chapter Two

IDENTIFYING THE SIGNS OF BULLYING

The first step towards dealing with any problem is usually identification. You need to identify if your child is a bullying victim, or if your kid is actually the bully in the scenario.

It's rare for a child to own up in either scenario since it's never easy to talk about how s/he is being mistreated at school nor is it equally simple to admit that s/he has been up to no good in the classroom.

Fortunately, there are quite a few telltale signs for either case to help you decide on the next course of action.

While there are a few bullied children who don't manifest any signs of being bullied, majority are bound to exhibit at least one of the following behavioral changes:

1) Unexplainable injuries. This may include scratches, cuts, bruises, or even cigarette burns on the skin. Be particularly wary when your child is keen on covering them up and/or can't seem to come up with a coherent explanation for their origin.

2) Missing or damaged personal belongings. If your child frequently shows up at home with torn or stained clothing, missing books, etc., it is a likely sign that s/he is a victim of bullying.

3) A loss of interest in going to school. Children or teenagers who make a lot of excuses to avoid going to school can sometimes do so in order to avoid an unpleasant encounter with a bully. This, coupled with a decline in your kid's academic performance (which could be due to his difficulty in focusing in class because of a bully's constant harassment), is a red flag for school bullying.

4) Drastic changes in eating habits. Children or teenagers can sometimes lose their appetite or limit their food intake if they

are bullied at school for their weight. On the other hand, if your kid always goes home hungry and binges at the dinner table, it could mean that s/he may be skipping lunch to avoid running into a bully or two.

5) Self-destructive behaviors. Episodes of self-harm, which may include cutting or binging/purging, are serious red flags.

If your child meets the following criteria, on the other hand, then s/he may be the ones inflicting pain upon his/her peers, and is thus due for a serious talking-to:

1) Unexplained new belongings or extra money. If your kid seems to have an extra influx of cash that doesn't seem to come from a new part-time job or from a recent birthday, then you might need to investigate if it came from shaking down a peer or classmate. If your child also sports new expensive equipment that appear to be personalized with someone else's name, then that too could mean that your kid got it by coercing someone into giving it up.

2) Having friends who bully others. Adolescents are at a highly impressionable age where their peers can easily sway them into doing things that aren't necessarily right. If your kid seems to be hanging out with a group of bullies a lot, then it might be time to sit him or her down for a talk.

3) Increased aggression levels. If your kid has been getting increasingly argumentative, defensive, or aggressive recently, there's a good chance that s/he might be doing worse to his/her weaker peers or classmates.

4) Frequent sessions with the principal or head teacher. If you find yourself being called to meetings with your child's teachers often to discuss your kid's hurtful behavior, chances are that your kid has been playing the bully for quite some time.

5) Frequent verbal or physical fights with others. Kids or adolescents who are frequently getting into confrontations with other people have a high likelihood

of turning out to be bullies, if they aren't such already.

Whichever end of the spectrum your child may fall on, try not to judge him or her too quickly.

As with most parenting issues, communication is key and whether they're the victim or the bully, your kid would still benefit from knowing that you would at least grant him or her the courtesy of a listening ear.

Once you've confronted and confirmed the issue at hand, then it would be time to take more decisive action, as the succeeding chapters will show.

Chapter Three

THE EFFECTS OF BULLYING

One reason why parents and educational institutions alike take such a proactive approach towards stomping out bullying is that its effects, when left unchecked, can reverberate throughout the entire community in devastating ways.

As with most traumatic incidents, bullying has both short-term and long-term effects. The short-term effects of bullying are often concentrated on the victim/s, and in some cases, even the bystander/s or witnesses can also suffer from being privy to the incident.

The more immediate consequences of bullying on victims include the following:

1) Heightened anxiety, especially around their peers.

2) A marked reluctance to attend school

3) A significant decline in academic performance

4) Feelings of anger and despair over how they seem to have lost control of their life

5) Episodes of depression or isolation

6) Increased emotional sensitivity or a distinct withdrawal from everyday life

7) Frequent nightmares

8) Suicidal thoughts. This particular effect can be quite dangerous, as plenty of shooting incidents in the US stem from bullying victims who wished to take out their tormentor/s, perceived or otherwise, before they took their own lives. The phenomenon has been so rampant recently that it spawned the term "bullicide."

Witnesses or bystander/s have also reported harboring feelings of fear, guilt, anger and helplessness shortly after inadvertently observing an incident of bullying.

The long-term effects of bullying, on the other hand affect the victim, the bully, the bystander/s, and the whole school. Those who were constantly bullied grow up to develop deep-seated feelings of inadequacy that could plague them throughout life, an inability to trust in other people, and mental illnesses like post-traumatic stress disorder (which gets in the way of them living normal lives).

Bullying victims, if left untreated or unaided, can also end up with an unhealthy zest for vengeance along with a psychopathic nature.

Kids who bully other kids, on the other hand, were more likely to engage in self-destructive behaviors like underage drinking and drug use, unprotected sexual activity (which makes them vulnerable to sexually-transmitted diseases and teenage pregnancy), and consorting with criminal behavior (e.g., vandalism, engaging in gang fights, etc.).

School bullies who were not subjected to proper counseling also had higher chances of manifesting antisocial personality disorders as adults, which enabled them to selfishly manipulate others for their own personal gain without any guilt. In a lot of cases, school bullies also turned out to be abusive spouses and parents.

Unwitting bystanders to bullying incidents can also start to live vicariously through the victims and feel the same sentiments of fear, anxiety, and isolation that the latter does in the long term.

Some end up turning to drugs or alcohol to dull these uncomfortable feelings, while others can display lack of enthusiasm for attending school. Feelings of powerlessness and guilt can also trouble them for quite some time.

If bullying incidents remain unattended to (or worse, ignored) by the school, then the entire institution gets impacted negatively. Any school that fails to create an atmosphere of safety and trust will quickly be subjected to the following effects:

1) Lack of parental trust in the school. This inevitably leads to some parents taking their children out of the institution and transferring them elsewhere.

2) A significant reduction in staff retention and satisfaction rates. Good teachers are in high demand, and they are unlikely to stay with an institution that fails to take proactive action when it comes to matters that involve the safety and wellbeing of the students.

3) Outright rebellion towards teachers and school staff. If the school authorities appear to be powerless and/or indifferent towards resolving widespread bullying, the students will eventually lose respect for them and might even defy them directly.

4) Lack of learning among the students. It is very difficult to focus on one's studies if there are constant threats to one's wellbeing hanging around. In this case, the very purpose of the school, which is to educate its pupils, is defeated by the presence of insidious and pervasive bullying.

5) The development of an environment of fear and disrespect. Bullies undermine the very notion of respect for one's peers and

authorities, and their presence only serves to engender terror amongst the student population.

Chapter Four

MYTHS ABOUT BULLYING

The bully is always the bigger person: Bullying is always about power and it is typically those who naturally have less of it that feel the need to do what they can to feel as though they have evened the odds. Especially with the increase of cyberbullying, bullies come in all shapes and sizes. When trying to determine if someone is a bully, don't judge a book by its cover, consider the actions that the other person is taking and make your decision based on those facts, not what they look like.

Bullying is a natural part of life: While it's true that most people experience an instance of bullying at least once in their lives, that does not mean that bullying is normal behavior. Bullies are socially deficient in other areas and accepting their existence goes a long way towards normalizing their place in our society.

There is one right way to deal with a bully: While conventional wisdom states that ignoring a bully's machinations is the easiest way to make sure they lose interest, in reality, every bully is different which means that, while sometimes ignoring them will be the appropriate response, other times you will need to turn the other cheek, alert an authority figure, or even fight back. The best approach to start with is to try ignoring their antics, followed by trying to befriend them if appropriate. Stooping to their level should only be attempted when all else has failed as it is equally likely to escalate things if used too soon.

Bullies are always popular: While John Hughes may feel differently, bullies are rarely actually at the top of the pecking order which means the root of most bullying is a desire for increased social status. The goal of a majority of bullying is to establish control over other people, a variation of the traditional social order. While most people who are traditional well liked would avoid stopping to bullying, bullies who are popular are especially malicious as their overall friendly nature can serve to prevent them from facing normal consequences.

Parents have little control when it comes to bullying: While it is well known that children who bullies are frequently abused at home, there are actually a wide variety of ways that parents can influence bullying scenarios. It is important for all parents to enforce the idea that it is wrong to force your will on others while at the same time making it clear that it is important to stand up for one's self in the face of oppression. Falling too far on one side of this line or the other can make it easier for children to either become bullies, or victims.

This doesn't mean that as a parent you need to intervene directly when bullying is involved as this can work against your goal in more ways than one. First of all, it is surprisingly likely for two parents whose children are involved in bullying to get into heated, possibly physical altercations themselves.

There is typically little leeway when children are involved and bullying characteristics could develop in the parent relationship as well. What's more, even if the parent promises to handle the issue, the results could possibly be detrimental to the other child who is simply a product of their environment. Generally, it is best to alert the school and let them handle the specifics.

Finally, it is important to take reports of bullying from your children seriously, making it seem as though their feelings on the topic are valid, before doing what you can to allow the child to handle the situation by themselves first, within reason.

Bullying is more common among boys: With the explosion of social media that took place in the 00s, the trend of boys being bullied more often than girls shifted dramatically in the other direction. It is more likely for girls to be cyberbullied while boys who are bullied are still often done so physically. This no doubt has something to do with the way adolescent boys and girls tend to develop a social hierarchy.

Physical bullying escalates from cyberbullying: While to parents, a physical altercation seems much more serious than the few dismissive texts sent back and forth beforehand, in reality, modern teens find more to connect with in the digital world than the physical one. It's a reverse of the old schoolyard standard, sticks and stones can break my bones put words can never hurt me; today however, it is the written word that is likely to last forever in an easily recallable format while a simple broken bone heals and is easily forgotten.

There is not much schools can do to stop it: With the escalation of cyberbullying in the past decade, a vast majority of states, 48 in all, have strict anti-bullying legislation on the books which strictly defines what is and what is not considered bullying and tasks the schools in question to report it promptly. It is the responsibility of the parents to understand their school's policies and to demand change where necessary.

Bullying is akin to conflict: This is a common misconception as to an outsider, the two can seem very similar. In reality, however, conflict occurs when two or more people with mutual animosity towards one another directly interact with one another. Bullying, on the other hand is typically one-sided and continues for a protracted period of time. As such, it is important to consider conflict resolution strategies separately from bullying resolution strategies as one will rarely work to mitigate the other.

When a child is bullied, others will rarely get involved: Here is one instance of things getting better as time goes one as current studies show that a majority of children don't think bullying is acceptable. This means that it is equally more likely that they will step in directly when they see someone being bullied or that they will go out of their way to tell a person in a position of authority.

Chapter Five

BULLYING MISCONCEPTIONS

Ever heard someone say that you can't do anything violent humanly! Well, misconceptions like these are common among people about bullying. To have a better understanding of bullying, it is important to know about the misconceptions attached to it.

First thing's first, bullying is an ultimate example of violence that is humanly possible for teenagers. Teasing someone has nothing do with bullying. Similarly, bullying is nowhere near **'Just teasing'**. It is important for teenagers as well as parents/guardians to understand that bullying is not a part of growing up. It is an unethical act of behaving badly with people. Like these, there are numerous misconceptions attached to bullying. Let's have a look at some of these:

ONLY BOYS ARE BULLIES

No! Girls can be a bully too. Girls and boys bully differently. Mean girls will be the first ones mocking you down in front of the school. They will not just talk about your grades and popularity, but will also body shame you. They will make your fun by sending you intimidating messages and texts. So, the next time you hear them say, **'She can't be the one because she is a girl'**. Tell them that they can be.

BULLY WILL GO AWAY IF AVOIDED/IGNORED

Avoidance is both a bliss and a cure. Let's say, not eating an ice-cream during the winter season will help you avoid catching a cold, but ignoring a bully and let him talk/gossip about you is not bliss. Next time someone says 'ignore bully', you better ignore the advice instead. Students engaged in the bullying behavior will not stop even if ignored. In fact, the biggest problem attached to teenage bullying is ignorance and staying quiet. The cases of bullying are becoming severe day by day because teenagers prefer ignoring and staying quiet.

It is just a consequence of Grade-Competition

Being marked failed in English test is not the only reason they insult you! Bullying is a learned behavior comprised of aggression and violence. It is not always about 'Grade competition'. Thereby, you need to have a close look at it to get to its source. Misreading grade competition teasing to actual bullying is the worst thing one can do. Bullying is not acceptable in any way.

BEING BULLIED BUILDS CHARACTER

Bullying is nowhere near character building; instead, it can encourage teenagers to contemplate suicide. Character building does not require public humiliation, insult, and violence. It is highly unethical to view bullying as a source of learning encouragement. You can never encourage someone through bullying them. So, beware next time, while trying to provoke them by bullying, you might end up hurting them.

HANDLE BULLYING ON THEIR OWN

The greatest misconception for teenagers is related to handling a bully. If a teenager knew how to handle bullying, they probably would have handled it by now. Teenagers are at a tender age where they need support and assistance in many aspects of their life. Teenagers avoid adult intervention in their matters which often leads to severe consequences. It is essential for teenagers to involve an adult as soon as possible. Involving an adult can help you in recovering/healing after the incident.

BULLY IS JUST AN ATTENTION SEEKER

They bully you because they need attention! No, a bully is a bully, and there is no excuse attached to it. Attention seeking individuals have no right to humiliate you and spread false rumors about you. Bullying will eventually increase if you don't give them attention. The core meaning of bully tells us that bullying is repeated rude behavior. Thus, there is no way a bully is going to do it just for gaining attention.

VULNERABILITY: WHO IS AT RISK?

Victims of bullying are at a vulnerable state because they become depressed, stressed, and anxious. Bullying can happen anywhere and at any time. Being in a victim state, teenagers can often feel challenged because it can negatively impact their psychological, emotional, and physical state. Typically, victims are teenagers who mostly lack social skills. Children belonging to a negative background also fall victim of bullying easily. Being physically weak or challenged can also put teenagers at the risk of being bullied. Bullying puts the victim at risk because it can cause greater social difficulties for them. The lack of social skills along with problem-solving abilities can lead to the development of complaints and headaches that form severe risk factors. The understanding of the victim state is effective in helping children become anti-bully. The risk of suicide increased with bullying among teenagers. Culturally, there are some dynamics that help in detecting victims. **So, who is at risk?** It is that one student who was also bullied by other student bullies in the past. The exposure to violent state makes them vulnerable because they are most likely to bully others in the future.

Another risk for bullies is linked with the teachers and staff members who intimidate or insult teenagers based on their performance in academics, sports, and extracurricular activities.

The risks for teenagers are further related to their isolation in schools. Many teenagers are at the risk of being bullied only because of their weak social problem-solving skills. The inability to handle social interactions can make teenagers fall in the trap of bullying.

Bystanders and Bystander Effect – What can they do?

Don't be just a Bystander!

Bullying is not just about bully and victim: in fact, it tells you the story of a bystander too. Bystanders must know about the bystander effect which is a social and psychological phenomenon. The bystander is not the person who witnessed you being bullied in a hallway; he is the one who saw you being bullied and did not do anything about it. The philosophy of human life doesn't just ask you not to be a victim or a bully but also tells you not to be a bystander too. A bystander is obliged to understand social paralysis which can have significant implications for teenagers.

Bullying situations usually involve people other than the victim and bully. Bystanders can play a major role in preventing bullying. A supportive bystander can tackle the situation. It would not be wrong today that the first step against bullying can be taken by the bystanders. In most cases, they can help teenagers in avoiding conflicts and fights. In person, fights will include many bystanders because it is related to public humiliation and insult of the bystander. In psychology, the idea of a bystander is drawn based on the bystander effect.

The effect will resist witnesses of the bullying situation from breaking social paralysis and helping the victim fighting against the bully. With the bystander effect, witnesses play their part in bullying. Staying quiet when someone is being bullied maybe not completely wrong, but up to some extent, it is indeed unethical. The bystander effect reflects the lack of interestedness among people toward ending bullying and helping the victim.

The bystander effect is usually related to ambiguity, diffusion of responsibility, and group cohesiveness. The effect and concept of a bystander for teenagers are different. The differences mainly arise due to the lack of understanding and awareness among them. There are many different ways in which bystanders can ensure in stopping bullying. Ultimately, many high school fights and bullying situations can be tackled with effective and timely intervention of the bystander. If you are a bystander of a bullying situation in your school, this is what you need to do:

Do not be a Gossipmonger!

Being a bystander, the principal step you can take is not to become a gossip machine. Don't go telling people about it just to enjoy a laughing experience. Make sure to avoid becoming the source of rumor spreading. The avoidance to become a gossipmonger will help the victim in retrieving confidence.

Be prepared to become a Proactive Witness

Looking at the situation, don't shy away from becoming a proactive witness. Play your part and share the truth with concerned parties, so that you make sure that you are not participating in any unethical incident. If possible, gather evidence in the form of a film or shots because they might be needed by the victim later. Being a bystander, this is your responsibility to avoid talking about the incident once it is over; just to make sure that you are not sharing news for fun with anyone.

Turn Laughter Back

Empathize! Do not go laughing like everyone else. Know how hard it will be for the victim who has been publically insulted or humiliated. In cyberbullying, you can play your role by not sharing explicit or personal content of the victim. Moving forward, you can also ask your friends, family, and acquaintances to stop sharing trolling posts against the victim. Your laugh or smirk will give all the confidence to the bully.

Spread Love!

Last but not least, be nice to everyone and spread the love. Make people aware that you respect and appreciate them. Talk to the victim and try empathizing because it will at least help them in healing.

Chapter Six

UNDERSTANDING BULLIES

You may think to yourself, "Who, in their right frame of mind, will even consider the possibility of bullying others?" It's wrong and unfair – shouldn't that be enough reason for people not to bully others?

There are reasons that seem legitimate to bullies, consciously or unconsciously, as to their behavior. For more power or popularity, bullies tend to impose their will on those that they feel are much weaker than them. One thing about bullies is that for all their self-proclaimed "toughness" and "righteousness", they don't take on people who they perceive to be at least equal to them in stature and power. Bullying is always making sure there's a weaker person to bully. Bullies hardly pick on someone they know can whoop their asses. Knowing that, victims of bullying may be the least popular, glasses-wearing, obese, frail, thin, culturally and ethnically unique, religious and homosexual people on the bully's side of the planet.

Bullies often bully others to make themselves feel good about themselves. And in order to continue enjoying such a feeling, the bully needs to perpetuate it continuously for a never-ending rush of power and prestige. So when the original object of bullying leaves, the bully compulsively looks for another one to pounce on in order to keep the feelings alive. And in many cases, bullies are some of the most insecure and sensitive people on earth and that they bully others to feel secure and superior. Aside from insecurity and feeling inferior, people bully others because:

-Vengeance: The bully may have been a bullied victim in the past too, whether by peers or family members. They may have been teased really badly to the point where they may have felt worthless or unimportant. This or similar feelings of being bullied may be their unconscious – or even conscious – way of getting even, albeit on other and weaker people.

-Loneliness: Bullies may also be doing it because they feel insignificant, unimportant, worthless and left out. Everyone needs attention and those who aren't noticed enough may transform into bullies later on. Why? Bullying can give them the feeling that they're significant and powerful, even if they already have friends.

-Domestic Problems: It's not unheard of that bullies are going through rough times at home. They may be experiencing verbal and physical abuse at home, among others, which may be affecting their minds and make them into emotionally aggressive people with fragile minds. In such cases, the bully is a victim as well. Even if they're not abused at home, living with a dysfunctional family, particularly one that lacks openness and affection, contribute to someone becoming a bully.

-Self-Esteem: Many bullies don't have a good view of themselves, e.g., not smart enough, unattractive or unworthy, and bullying makes them feel more confident about themselves. Remember how your mother would tell you to look at less fortunate people to appreciate what you have? In a rather twisted way, that's the case with bullies who have low self-esteem. They make others feel inferior by bullying so they can feel superior and have higher self-esteem.

-Jealousy: As with low self-esteem, bullying makes a bully feel better when jealous of another person who makes them feel inferior or one-upped. This type of bullying may be more specific or particular to a person of interest rather than being generally bullying others.

-Peer Influence: In most cases, bullies like to roll together like birds of the same feather. As such, they tend to become what they are part of. Often times, the desire to hang out with other bullies is for "coolness" or for security, in case the people they bully fight back. They feel stronger and safer when they're in a group of like-minded people.

-Ego: Although many bullies are hurting people themselves, some aren't. They're just proud as hell with egos the size of Texas. They're just so arrogant as to think they're God's greatest gift to mankind and until someone else smacks some sense into their heads, such a belief and behavior will continue to perpetuate.

-Needs To Impress: Part of having a big ego may be the need for other people's admiration.

There's really nothing wrong with feeling that way but the problem lies in how to be admired. Bullies normally are void of any special talents or personalities to attract people so what they do is simply push people around – that becomes their special talent or skill, which makes them feel special and admired.

-Unique View Of You: Bullies normally pick their victims based on certain characteristics that they deem as special. Hence, they view their victims as unique or sees them in ways most others don't. It may be that they view their victims' sexuality, physical defects or race as inferior or despicable and hence the aggression towards them. They may either let their reason for bullying others be known or not but it doesn't matter – they're still bullying others and that's wrong regardless.

-Need For Control: Bullies often bully others who they feel are weaker because they have an overwhelming need for experiencing a great sense of control over their lives and by controlling others through bullying, they believe they're able to do that. These people are usually hotheaded and impulsive and people who are not brave enough to stand up for themselves are fair game to them.

-It's Rewarded: Believe it or not, bullying may be a way for bullies to get rewards that are important for them, even if they may not be aware of it. For example, school bullies who often pick on weaker kids for their lunch or allowances receive the rewards of delicious food and money to spend just by intimidating or harassing others. Great rewards for practically no work. The popularity and benevolence often associated with being a bully is another reward that they love to get through bullying. In other words, the behavior is encouraged by rewards.

-Inability To Control Emotions: Some people simply can't control their frustration and anger to the point they resort to hurting other people. With such inability to manage feelings, small incidents and disappointments can cause such people to tick so violently as to react with physical, relational or verbal aggression. An example of this is when a person accidentally bumps into a bully. Even after apologizing, the bully would beat up the other person as a "consequence" of bumping into him.

Bullies may have logical reasons for their

behavior but no amount of such will ever justify it. It's a very serious issue that won't just drift away – it needs to be addressed together by the necessary parties such as administrators, teachers, parents, management and government agencies, among others. With the right tools and techniques, victims of bullying can be taught how to handle it well and bullies' minds can be changed.

Chapter Seven

CHILD PREVENTION

Given the impact bullying has on children and how it can forever change their lives, mostly for the worst, it's important that we are able to address bullying from the grassroots even before it grows into a full-fledged monster.

PREVENTION

Prevention is always better than cure. As such, one of the best ways to stop bullying is to keep it from happening – prevention. There are several ways to do this: awareness campaigns, educating students, punishment system and an anti-bullying policy.

Preventing bullying even before it rears its ugly head can attack the problem on different fronts. Prevention measures can be directed towards fostering a situation where there's zero tolerance for bullying, behavioral suggestions for potential bullies or even giving them outlets where they can pour out their feelings and thoughts that may lead to bullying, and equipping potential bullying victims avoid such situations or themselves prevent it. There are a number of ways that parents can work with their children to ensure that they have a proper idea of what to do when bullied while still not becoming bullies themselves.

Display the appropriate types of relationships: The single most important thing that parents can do when it comes to ensuring that their children don't grow up to be either bullied or bullies is to emphasize the importance of loving relationships as well as the fact that displaying power is not an effective way to gain social status. As such it is important to never use physical power or influence when disciplining a child or else they will learn that it is okay to be overpowered by others, or even worse, that overpowering others is the best way to get what they want. It is important to always encourage open discourse when it comes to solving problems with a child so they learn that the best way to deal with any situation is with words.

Ensure your child enjoys social settings:

Children who are loners are more likely to either become bullied or bully others in the long run. It is important to model the idea to your child that being with other people is a natural and enjoyable thing to do.

Be confident: Parents who back down in order to avoid conflict are teaching their children the same thing. While this will result in adults who don't make waves unnecessarily, it will also result in adults who are less likely to stand up for themselves when they are in fact being pushed around unfairly. It is important to only assert yourself when necessary, however, as being too aggressive can easily send the wrong message. This also goes for those who use self-deprecating remarks about themselves, generally as a defense mechanism. Parents who don't have strong self-images will pass along the message that this is an acceptable way to live to their children as well.

Teach your children to assert themselves: It is important that at an early age each child be taught how to assert their rights while at the same time understanding that there are times when the needs of the many outweigh the needs of the few. The key is to teach them how to assert their opinions in an effect way. Consider phrases such as:

- Now it is my turn.
- Please stop what you are doing.
- Keep your hands to yourself.
- That's hurts, stop it.
- *Please call me by my name instead.*

Try roleplaying: Bullies typically choose their targets based on the response they receive based on verbal threats or name calling. A desired response gives the bully the power they are looking for while at the same time guaranteeing they will continue their assault, possibly more severely than before. As such, it is important to pretend with your child and walk them through possible taunts they might receive as well as appropriate responses for them to reply with.

In this scenario it is important that children understand exactly how bullies operate and how to hide their emotions while appearing to remain in control. Explain that the bully is trying to incense the situation and the best way to win is to not engage and instead work on diffusing the situation as quickly as possible. When practicing it is important to ensure that your child always retains eye contact while speaking in a strong, authoritative tone, practice daily until your child can perform perfectly on cue every time. Providing your child with the right mindset will go a long way to making them a much less likely target for bullies.

Explain the nature of fear: Children frequently have a negative view of fear and find it a shameful emotion. When it comes to dealing with bullies, it is important that your child understands that there is no shame in being afraid, it is how they respond to the fear that is important. It is important to push through minor things that cause you fear in order to grow but fear also lets you know when a scenario or situation has escalated out of control. Instill in your child the importance of knowing the difference and to seek out an authority figure if things look as though they may get out of hand.

Show your child that it is important to intervene when others are being bullied: While teaching your child how to avoid being bullied is nice, teaching them to help others who are being bullied is a strong step towards creating a future with fewer bullies tomorrow than there are today. It is important to encourage them to strive to remove the victim form harm's way before turning the crowd against the bully. As most bullies are motivated by a desire for social acceptance, this reversal will cause them to lose confidence. It is important to, again, stress the importance of contacting an authority figure when the situation requires, safety should always be presented as a primary concern.

Policies

One good way to prepare a school for handling and neutralizing the threat of bullying is through policies that clearly define what bullying is, prohibiting it in school and establishing the appropriate consequences for such behavior. When bullying is clearly defined, it's more easily identified or recognized as it's happening and can be clearly distinguished from motivation, discipline and constructive criticism, which are activities that may be confused for bullying. The policy itself needs to be clear and based on good research to avoid being too broad and general, which may make students and teachers feel uncomfortable to say anything that isn't "nice" believing it may be taken against them as "bullying". For example, if an anti-bullying policy doesn't clearly categorize what makes for bullying, the basketball team's coach may be afraid to pick the best players for fear that cutting off the worst performing ones may become a basis for scorned parents to file a "bullying" complaint.

Another key characteristic that a good anti-bullying policy should contain is the explicit enumeration of major kinds of bullying, i.e., verbal, physical, cyber and social, among others. It is also important that the policy should also include bullying of those that aren't normally considered as "bully-able" like popular students, teachers, staff and other members of the school's administration.

Consequences

A well-written and detailed anti-bullying policy needs to have a set of consequences that are hopefully good enough to dissuade bullies from doing their thing. Having this helps victims know that they'll be treated fairly and securely in order to encourage them to come out and report their bullying experiences. More than just having a solid set of bullying consequences, the policy should be applied consistently and fairly, without fear or favor, in order for it to have any effect on potential bullies.

Home Education

The nature and perception of bullying has changed a lot over the years and while schools can come up with the best anti-bullying policies, it isn't enough because bullying can happen outside of school. The most encompassing way to prevent bullying is within the family. It's because most people's behaviors are shaped at home – what they see and experience in it. If the school says bullying sucks but is a constant regular attraction at home, guess what? The kid will believe his reality at home. Their role models speak louder than school regulations. More than just punishments, which can only go so far, children need role models to emulate and truth is, the home is the best place for such role models.

While it's hard and time consuming to effectively communicate a community than a family when it comes to things like bullying, objections to family education makes it even harder. This is because of the issue of privacy and confidentiality, which makes people resent and reject any forms of suggestion for change. Many parents would simply be too proud to admit if they're raising their children wrong. But if there's no change in the family environment where say, dad bullies mom or brother bullies sister, it will eventually cascade out into the school and the general community.

At home, parents can keep bullying from happening by teaching and modeling. They can explicitly explain to their kids what characterizes bullying and how's it different from constructive criticism and motivating, among other things, and teach them what behaviors are acceptable and unacceptable in the family. And most importantly, parents should reinforce their teachings with action. It's been said that faith without works is dead and parents' actions can either make or break whatever they teach their kids about bullying.

Other Prevention Measures

Appropriate intervention coupled with supervision can go a long way in arresting ongoing bullying's, including teaching and empowering the victims – both actual and potential – to assert themselves. It includes teaching or encouraging victims and potential victims to avoid circumstances where they'll be bullied.

A good example of this would be a kid who's being bullied because he stinks – literally. The reason for his being bullied is simply hygiene so encouraging and teaching him to practice good hygiene can help make the bullying go away and at the same time, increase his self-esteem because doing so will make him more attractive physically and scent-wise.

Consider also a kid who keeps on wearing a Yankees shirt in an area that's predominantly Red Sox. That's a surefire way to encourage others, i.e., the predominantly Red Sox fans, to bully him. By respecting their territory, he avoids being bullied. In cases like this, prudence is the better part of valor.

Then of course, there are situations where the appropriate thing to do is learn how to assert one's self, especially if he or she isn't doing anything wrong or embarrassing. One way is through self-defense, physical or verbal. Many times, bullying thrives in the absence of resistance, like evil does when no good person acts.

BULLYING IN PROGRESS

There are situations that bullying can't be perfectly prevented and so, intervention in an ongoing one is necessary to stop it. Here are ways ongoing school bullying's can be stopped.

School Administration

School administrators and teachers must be cognizant that bullying isn't just limited to the cliché areas such as playgrounds, bathrooms, school buses and hallways – it can also happen through gadgets and online. They should also be able to clearly communicate to the students that there's a world of difference between telling school authorities of an ongoing bullying and merely tattling.

Teachers need to be both vigilant and courageous enough to spot an ongoing bullying incident and step in to intervene and stop it, report it and participate in the school administration's investigation of the incidents. Such investigations, however, shouldn't involve both parties – the bully and the victim – jointly participating in meetings as this can be intimidating to the victim and keep him or her from freely telling the truth.

Parents and Students

It's not just the task of the school administration to handle bullying – it's also the responsibility of the parents. They should actively participate in any anti-bullying campaigns that their schools are conducting. Without their active involvement, such campaigns simply won't work.

Students must be encouraged to inform their parents when they're being bullied as well as orienting them on ways are being bullied in cyberspace. How can they be encouraged? The school's administration and the students' parents can teach them exactly how to act when they're bullied or when they see others being bullied and encourage them to take action against bullying. Even older students can be younger ones' mentors about how to avoid being bullied on cyberspace.

Encouraging students to ask for help when being bullied may be a challenging task. How challenging? The 2012 Indicators of School Crime and Safety's numbers revealed that in more than half or 60% of bullying incidents, adults weren't notified. Children simply refuse to tell their parents or any adult for that matter about their bullying experiences for several reasons:

- -Reporting bullying incidents makes children even more helpless, which is how they already fell when bullied. By not telling adults, they feel that they regain lost control. Reporting incidents, they feel, will make them appear either a tattletale or fearful, which they think will worsen the bullying even more.

- -They also fear that bullies may get back at them even more for reporting the incidents.

- -Because being bullied is one of the most humiliating experiences ever, children may not be comfortable with their parents or other adults knowing what's being said about them – true or not – and how their being treated in school. Part of this fear may be the parents or adults themselves –

that they'll be judged as weak or humiliating for being bullied and not being able to stand up to it.

- -Bullied kids may also feel socially rejected as a result of such – that no one really cares for them nor understands them.

- -Lastly, social proof is very important for children and they probably fear that reporting bullying incidents will make their peers look at them unfavorably and reject them.

Behavioral Expectations of Adults

Students should be afforded a learning environment of safety and security. Part of this are coaches and teachers explicitly informing and reminding their students that in their school, bullying is not and will never be tolerated and that engaging in such behavior will result in punishments. Having both the students and their parents or guardians read and sign copies of the school's anti-bullying policy can help both parties truly understand the seriousness of bullying.

For students who are socially awkward, i.e., find it hard to making friends or adjusting socially, the school administration can foster opportunities to do so or give them tasks to do during breaks to minimize the chances of them feeling isolated and becoming fair game for bullying.

Bullied Students' Parents

One of the parents' biggest responsibilities is to regularly monitor or observe their children for bullying red flags. This is because of the reasons I enumerated earlier for children not opening up to adults about their bullying experiences. When they notice one of the red flags enumerated in Chapter 5 manifesting in their kids, they shouldn't just tell them to suck it up and let it go – they need to encourage their kids to openly talk about it with them and be assured they won't be judged negatively for doing so. The more the child opens up, the better the chance the parents and the school administration can take corrective measures to stop an ongoing bullying.

Another way that parents of bullied children can help their kids is by empowering them – teach them how to handle bullying well. The school administration won't be able to completely monitor and rescue their students from incidences of bullying and as such, it's best to equip them to be able to handle it themselves. One of the best ways to do this is by role-playing practices at home where the children can practice avoiding, ignoring and standing up to bullies. Another good thing to teach children is being able to identify friends and teachers who can help them when they're bullied.

Technological Boundaries

Children should also be taught about cyberbullying and not to participate in threatening emails either by responding to such or forwarding them. Parents can do well to add up their kids in their Facebook and other social media accounts and install the appropriate controls on their computers. One way of discouraging them from improper use of social media is by limiting their access at home to a single, family-use computer and placing that computer in a very exposed place such as the living room so they can be easily monitored.

Giving children the latest advanced cellular

phones may not be a good idea because they can easily access the Internet through it and take photos and post them on their social media accounts, which can make them fair game for cyberbullying. Any threatening messages should be reported to the appropriate authorities.

Bullies' Parents

The parents of bullies have a very significant role to play in stopping an ongoing bullying. It's possible that their children who bully others are simply not aware or adept at reading social signs and do not know that what they're doing hurts other children as well. As such, they should sit their child down and educate him or her about the implications of their behavior, including possible legal consequences.

Modeling, as mentioned earlier, is one of the most powerful ways to show children that bullying is unacceptable. When children see their parents walk the talk, chances are they won't bully others or stop bullying them. More is caught than taught and action speaks louder than words. Action also reinforces words. When children are exposed to their parents' or siblings' aggressive behavior or if they're too restricted or constricted at home, the chances of them bullying or continuing to bully others are much higher.

Another way parents of bullies can help their bully kids drop it is by looking for and addressing low self-esteem issues. As I mentioned earlier, bullies can also be suffering from low self-esteem. Parents are in the best position to help their children enjoy higher self-esteem. To the extent they're able to make their children feel loved and accepted without having to be popular or accomplished, chances are that the desire for bullying will stop.

Bullied Students

The best option for bullied students is to report any incidence of bullying to their parents, teachers or any trusted adult. Often times, bullying's go unreported for the reasons I outlined earlier. In particular, reporting cyber-bullying to their parents may result in the confiscation of their smartphones or tablets, hence the reluctance to report. Better to be bullied than go offline. The funny thing is that if the parents find out about it from other sources, the more they'll want to take away their gadgets.

But if the kids come clean, then the parents will be more open to letting them keep those devices because by coming clean, they're convinced that their child is serious about addressing the problem and that they're responsible enough to report such.

Bullied students should also take into consideration that the best way to handle bullying incidents is to have responsible adults – parents and teachers – handle it. But since even the best laid plans sometimes go to waste, the last resort is standing up for one's self. But regardless, bullying back is not an option – ever. Wrongs can be never be made right by another wrong. When asserting one's self, the best route is to calmly tell the one doing the bullying to stop or just walk away. Physical defense is only acceptable when physically attacked or harassed already and should only be the last resort.

Another way to keep bullying at bay is avoiding being alone. It's because bullies often prey on those that they feel are helpless. When in a group, bullies will have to subdue more people, which they'll perceive to be either a losing proposition that will only lead to humiliation or something that's not worth the effort. Either way, it can go along way in preventing bullying.

Chapter Eight:

FINDING SUPPORT FROM PEOPLE AROUND

Having someone trustworthy around is the best defense system against cyberbullying. This support system will definitely help by doing simple things – encourage the victim to move on and try activities that will divert the victim's attention. By helping the victim forget the pains caused by cyberbullying, he is likely to recover. These are some things that can be done to move on from cyberbullying completely:

- For a while, do some social media fasting. Or it might be best if the victim will veer away from all forms of technology – at least until he is ready again. There is no harm in taking the necessary break from laptops, tablets, iPad, mobile phones, and the World Wide Web. There are many other ways to connect with true friends. While technology can help you connect with friends, it may not be 100 percent necessary.

- Find other people who manifest the same kind of interests and values. It is easy to make friends from a group which has a lot of things in common with you. Learn from them new things and have fun with them.

- Express how you feel and share your insights about cyberbullying. Encourage the victim to speak up. It is important to do a check on how the victim feels about what he recently went through. Additionally, a lot of realizations are made by merely sharing how you feel and think.

- Realize the reasons for being more confident. Dwell on your strengths and turn your weaknesses into opportunities. By being more confident, you can significantly reduce levels of stress.

This Section Is for the Parents and Teachers

Usually, kids tend to hide their feelings from their teachers and parents even if they are already experiencing too much pain. They are reluctant because of fear of being scolded or of being ostracized by fears – even if it is not their fault at all. They are also afraid that telling the cyberbullying incident will lead to being put away from gadgets forever. So as parents or teachers, never tell children that their access to all forms of technology will be withdrawn.

In order to prevent cyberbullying from happening before it even begins, the following steps might be helpful:

- Teach kids to refrain from passing along messages coming from a cyberbully.

- Encourage kids to speak up against bullying and tell them that it is okay to be vocal against cyberbullying.

- Tell your kid's friend that cyberbullying is wrong.

- If a person is detected and confirmed to be a cyberbully, block your child's communication with him. If your child receives any message from the cyberbully, teach him to erase those messages even without reading any of them.

- Teach your kid not to post any personal information in order to protect his privacy. Some information that should not be posted online include: full name, complete address, home phone number, mobile number, name of parents, name and address of the school, number of the credit card, and other important details. It is also important to educate your kid not to share information about his friends.

- Remind your kid not to share passwords. But for his sake, tell him that you need to be informed of his password so that you can guide him and protect him at all times.

- Encourage kids to be vocal about his online persona and share his online adventures and misadventures with you.

- Tell your kids not to put anything that he will regret later on.

- Teach your kid not to post anything on

his social networking site if he is too happy, too hungry, or too angry.

- Think twice before posting anything. Do not post anything that you will not be able to say personally.

In order to be able to fully monitor the child's use of technology, here are some tips that are worth following. Do these in the name of his protection:

- Your home computer should be positioned in an area that is often frequented by adults. This way, you will know how it is being used. Refrain from giving your child an access to a mobile gadget in connecting to the Internet (like smart phone, tablet, or laptop. Ban all devices inside the bedroom.

- Limit your child's access to data since it is necessary for him to have his own smart phone. There are providers that can limit the text messaging within a given window of time. So, when he is already home, turn off SMS service.

- Personally, set up the filters of the

computer of your child. Install software that needs to be used to track software use. This way, you can easily block websites and web contents that are not appropriate for your child. This will also be helpful in monitoring the activity of your child online.

- This has already been mentioned previously, but it is worth mentioning again. You need to get the password of your children in their social networking websites. Also, make an effort to learn the language that your kids are using when drafting their text messages and instant messages, especially the acronyms.

- Get to know every single person that your kid is interacting to in the online world. If possible, go over his address book and friends list. Personally, ask your kid about his online friends.

Finally, and most importantly, be the most trusted adult so that your child will not hesitate to share anything with you. Be cool and never be too nagging. Reassure them that no one can hurt him unless he allows them to. More importantly, ur kid that you will protect him by all

Chapter Nine

WHY DO TEENAGERS BULLY?

Why is it that in high school, teenagers feel like bullying their colleagues or juniors? Bullying is not just that an accidental incident that occurs in the hallway during lunch break when two students get into a fight over a casual school matter. Actually, constantly making fun of people who appear to be a bit different from the majority in the crowd is what's known as bullying.

It is also to make people feel vulnerable, low, and insulted based on their appearance, race or religion, behavior, and social status. Treating people badly based on materialistic factors like their social image, popularity, and fame is also a significant part of bullying. In most of America, Canada, and the UK, bullying among children usually occurs due to the differences in race and religion.

People belonging to different cultures or having different religious beliefs are looked down upon and treated poorly. To have a better understanding of bullies and bullying, it is imperative to explore the reasons that make children emotionally, physically, or verbally abusive. The research about the reasons leading to bullying behavior among children found that it is often linked with the bully's victim state. For example, if a child is being a bully or abusive in school, there are high chances that he/she has seen aggressive behavior at home or somewhere else. Surprising! **Isn't it?**

Bullies themselves might have experienced emotional or physical abuse at some point in their life. Children often bully others into feeling in control and powerful. Psychologically, bullying is a way of coping with anger and unhappiness among children. Most likely, it is the way children deal with peer pressure imposed on them. It helps children in hiding their self-esteem issues because they appear as cold and unemotional, while they mock you down in front of everyone.

They believe that no-attachment and low emotions will make them superior. Self-esteem and confidence issues among children occur as the driving force for them that belittles their empathy for others. Ultimately, due to the lack of empathy, children end up abusing others. It gives them a false sense of power and focus. Children with low social skills face a hard time getting along with others and forming friendships. Such children abuse others to hide their insecurities and issues under cold and rude behavior.

WHO GETS BULLIED? WHAT IS WRONG WITH THEM?

What is wrong with me? This is the constant question that pops up in children's mind when faced by abuse of any kind. Children who are mocked or ridiculed by others often fall into a trap that makes them believe that they are not good enough. What these children need to hear is that NOTHING is wrong with you. It is always the fault of the one who is bullying you. No one in the world deserves to be treated badly.

No one can tell you that you are not good enough. Nothing in the world can reason or justify bullying of any kind in any way. Regrettably, statistics revealed by Trinity College Dublin shows that 30% of children reported their involvement in bullying in one way or the other. As per the survey conducted by Trinity College Dublin, 31% of primary and approximately 16% of secondary school students have been bullied at some point in their lives.

So, who are the victims?

Approximately, every child is the potential target of bullying. There are no fine criteria set by bullies which victims have to qualify to be bullied and degraded: instead, anyone and everyone can fall in the trap of bullying. Mostly, children who are weak, insecure, sensitive, or different from their peers fall victim of bullying. Victims are the ones who face insult and abuse from the bullies. These teenagers encounter aggressive behavior as well as violence whenever they face a bully.

Due to their constant exposure to violence and bullying, they become emotionally withdrawn. In different cases, victims respond differently. For example, some teenagers will stay quiet due to their shy nature whereas some teenagers will become self-contained; both are equally tragic. Victims have a high chance of becoming mentally disturbed, especially due to exposure, social isolation, and public humiliation.

HOW TO SPOT BULLYING?

We can do something against bullying only when we are able to spot it. What it looks like? When it occurs? How it starts and where it ends? We need to know everything before thinking about solving this problem. First of all, spotting bullying is easy because we all must have seen or encountered it at some point in our lives, but do we know about the signs and symptoms that can help in determining the effects of bullying on teenagers? Let's look at these symptoms:

Emotional Signs

A bullied child will reflect emotional instability

There are some signs that can help people in reading child bullying. Emotionally, bullied children are not stable because they are exposed to so much disgust and hate that they start talking negatively about themselves. The most common emotional sign indicating child abuse or bullying is **isolation**. Yes, isolation increases with an increase in bullying.

Look for the teenager preferring isolation over the company because he/she must have faced some kind of humiliation at some level. On the other hand, anxiety is another important indicator of abuse or bullying among children. Teenagers often reflect unsubtle changes in emotions and behaviors after being exposed to some kind of bullying.

It can make children afraid because it's scary and unsettling. Often, children complain about trouble in sleeping. These emotional symptoms can also relate to low self-esteem or self-confidence among teenagers, which itself is the end result of bullying. Parents and guardians need to keep track of the emotional status of children because being exposed to bullying is reflected in their behaviors.

School Problems

I don't want to go to School!

If being bullied at school, the first reaction of the child will be to miss school. The increase in the child's refusal to go to school can tell you a lot about the schools' environment. Expression of hate or fear of going to school can depict the level of bullying occurring at school. Children will avoid making public appearances or refuse to call friends over for a hangout.

This change in hanging out routine and the preference of children to stay indoors can help us in reading their exposure to bullying. In most cases, children will not be able to perform well as a result of bullying, which can affect their academic performance. School problems like poor performance, low grades, and reduced interest in sports can also relate to the exposure of a child to bullying. After being bullied, it becomes challenging for teenagers to attend school because it makes them anxious. Missing practice, school trips, and canceling group projects become common for such teenagers. Children with these symptoms need help with bullying!

Physical Signs

Unexplained physical injuries like torn clothing and bruises are enough for telling that the child has faced bullying at school. Keep a close check on your child's physical state. Physical signs not only relate to the victim, but they also relate to missing or damaged belongings. Teenagers' belongings being damaged or missing can also show that he/she has faced bullying. The physical health of the child along with his/her belonging can form strong evidence for bullying.

Similarly, if a teenager constantly complains about unstable health, lack of motivation, and low interest, it is a high time to check his/her surroundings. Child neglecting cleanliness and personal grooming can also help in detecting uncertainty. The way teenagers behave after facing physical abuse or bullying can turn out to be alarming. To know the emotional impact and influence of child abuse, one needs to closely look at their physical response to different situations. It is an old proverb that says **'Children will do what they see you doing'**. Bullied children have high chances of becoming violent in their life later.

Chapter Ten

VICTIM ON THE BULLY

For children, bullying can make them lose interest in studying especially if the bullying happens in school because studying is associated with it – the place where he or she is bullied. As a result, it can lead to serious drops in academic performance and if the academic performance is already poor to begin with, getting kicked out of school or dropping out from it. Moreover, bullying kids may result in physical injuries and mental issues.

Anxiety and depression at such a very young age may also be a result of being bullied. I mean, who wouldn't be, especially if the kid's personality is neither aggressive nor strong? They'll end up sad and lonely and may even experience sleeping and eating disorders on top of becoming disinterested in the activities they normally love to do.

Worse, it may just end the kid's life as with Ryan Patrick Halligan. The media is rife with stories of kids committing suicides as a result of being bullied. Equally bad is the tendency to go the other route – revenge. Many of the school shooting incidents were acts of revenge by kids who were bullied and who wanted to take the power back and get even with their tormentors. Such retaliation is often referred to as "bullicide". If you look at the 1990s, more than half of the shootings were related to bullying – retaliation.

Children who have the tendency to behave violently are often bullies. If they continue bullying others unimpeded or without consequences, it will only escalate because bullying makes them feel powerful and power is intoxicating, making bullies want to up the ante even more. Worse, they may even continue being so as full-grown adults.

Kids who bully others have a higher propensity to:

- -Participate in other risky behavior;
- -Instigate vandalism and fights, which can

cause them to either drop out or be kicked out from school;

- -Become sexually promiscuous at an early age with an increased risk for being sexually abused and acquiring sexually transmitted diseases; and

- -Grow into spouses that abuse their partners and kids.

Short term signs of bullying

While bullying can cause a number of long-term issues that those around the victim need to be aware of, it can also lead to a number of serious issues that need to be resolved as quickly as possible to ensure that they do not become more pronounced with time.

(For the Victim) Depression: This is a big one to watch out for, though it can be difficult to pick up pronounced differences in teens who are already naturally quiet and withdrawn. Depression is more likely to be related to instances of cyberbullying which typically include more of a feeling of hopelessness and tend to typically last much longer than physical bullying encounters and typically increase in intensity over time as well. Signs of depression include:

- outbursts of sadness as well as anger and irritability that is prolonged.
- A loss of interest in hobbies and interests.
- Apparent apathy towards social contact, even with friends.
- Noticeable, sudden change in habits or patterns.
- Noticeable, sudden change in eating patterns or habits.
- Complaints of exhaustion.
- Expression of feelings of hopelessness, helplessness, worthlessness or guilt.
- A lack of focus.
- Sudden unexplained (or poorly explained) aches and pains.
- A sudden interest in suicide/talk indicating potential harmful courses of action.

(For the Victim) Loss of self-confidence: Belief in

one's self is important for long term success, especially for those who are young and still making their way in the world. Having belief in oneself can often make the difference between success and failure. If you notice your child suddenly beginning to experience a drastic variation in their general level of self-confidence, bullying may be to blame. Signs of low self-confidence include.

- They seem to become unreasonably nervous and fidgety in social situations.

- They immediately back down when presented with conflict.

- They adopt an eye-catching clothing or physical affectation.

- They seem to take all criticism to heart.

- It is difficult to get them to express an opinion.

- They always seem indecisive.

- They always deflect compliments.

- They give up as soon as things stop going their way.

- They are always comparing themselves to others.

- Their posture suddenly becomes much worse.

(For the Victim) Issues sleeping: Even if they won't discuss it, being aware of your child's sleeping habits can go a long way towards letting you know if they are being victimized by bullies. Roughly 45 percent of children bullied reported issues relating to amount of sleep or quality of sleep while 25 percent complained of persistent nightmares. What's more, this pattern of poor sleep can stick with children for years if not decades. In addition, 75 percent of the time when nightmares persisted for a prolonged period of time, bullying was revealed to be at least part of the problem.

(For the Victim) Issues wetting the **bed:** While wetting the bed is a relatively common occurrence in children under the age of 7, doing so with increased regularity or after a prolonged period of nightly bladder control, especially in older children, can often be a sign of extreme stress, anxiety or psychological trauma such as that brought on by having to deal with a bully, especially for the first time. Regardless of why the issue is now occurring, it is important to let the child know that it is not their fault and that it is an involuntary reaction. The reason for the bedwetting in these types of scenarios is often linked to the response of taking comfort in food during times of stress which can lead to a change in diet which can also cause the condition.

(For the Victim) Physical conditions not caused directly by the bullying: The stress a person being bullied feels at the prospect of yet another conflict with their bully can be enough to cause numerous physical conditions, not directly caused by any physical bullying that may be occurring. Dizziness, headaches and stomachaches can all be caused simply by the feelings of intense stress that may occur as a result of prolong periods of abuse. As such, a sudden influx of these symptoms, without their maturation into an actual illness should always be considered a cause for possible bullying concerns.

Long term effects of bullying

When not caught in a timely enough fashion, and if the results of the initial confrontations are not worked through in an appropriate manner, those who experience severe enough bullying can experience a variety of long-term effects that can have severe, perhaps life long, consequences.

The most common two are anxiety and depression that lasts far beyond the length of the bullying session, eventually becoming chronic disorders that will haunt the victims of bullying for the rest of their lives. Either one or both of these issues can make everything from finding new hobbies, exercising, working and even sleeping difficult or, in severe cases impossible. This also goes for forming meaningful relationships either interpersonal or romantic.

Even those who escape either depression or anxiety oftentimes have a permanently impacted self-image and they may never be able to see an accurate reflection of themselves anywhere. It can also lead to an inability in the victim to trust themselves in any high risk/high reward scenarios likely leading to a less successful life overall.

Post-traumatic stress disorder

While it might seem extreme, enough people have come forward with a variation of complex post-traumatic stress disorder, specific to bullying, that a detailed analysis of just what constitutes it is readily available. Those who are now suffering from bullying related PTSD tend to exhibit the following symptoms:

Periods of extreme chronic fatigue because their flight or fight response is always active whenever they are in a space that is not considered completely safe.

- A particularly intense need to express vitriolic anger when it comes to injustice either real or perceived.

- An extreme, driving desire to be validated, recognized, understood or acknowledged.

- A strong reticence to avoid talking or thinking about the subject of bullying.

- A strong sense of the difference between justice and revenge with a stong focus on the former over the latter.

- Rarely objective when it comes to slights both real or perceived with a tendency to vacillate between anger and forgiveness.

- Emotionally fragile.

- A feeling of numbness that extends beyond a lack of emotion to a physically deadening of sensation.

- A tendency towards clumsiness.

- A tendency towards absentmindedness.

- A strangely acute ability to judge the amount of time which has passed or the amount of distance traveled.

- An extreme sense of commitment to the environment either locally or on a broader scale.

- A focus on living a healthy lifestyle including the adoption of a vegan or vegetarian diet. Red meat is specifically avoided.

- A pervasive need to justify every thought or action or to prove self-worth when surrounded by friends or loved ones.

- A keen sense of when they are being victimized or betrayed by another person either real or imagined.

- Visions of potentially violent scenarios.

- Unwarranted feelings of being unlovable, unlikeable, worthless, rejected or unwanted.

What's more, they can experience a unique form of survivor's guilt which causes them to not want to report the bully in the moment, despite knowing that it might lead to viable repercussions. Later on however, these feelings lead to a strong desire to act out against the bully, typically couched in a desire to help others avoid future abuse.

The guilt also manifests itself in a hyper advanced sense that others in the world are unhappy which means that the victim of the bullying feels as though they can never be happy as well. This is also seen in their commitment to helping those who are under stress, even if they brought the situation upon themselves. Those with this type of survivor's guilt are also known to particularly identify with the suffering of others. They may also feel extreme and unwarranted negative responses to merit-based award.

Both bully and bullied

Those who are both bullied by others and then

become bullies themselves are more likely than either bullies or the bullied to end up displaying a wider variety of limitations throughout their lives. Bullying behavior is often learned at a young age which leads to anxiety and depression that is unlikely to improve as they move into the alternate position to the one in which they started. The variety of psychiatric disorders they are likely to express is also much greater than those who were only in a single camp.

These issues include things like panic disorder, generalized anxiety disorder, and agoraphobia. In addition, they were more likely than either bullies or their victims to have harmful thoughts related to self-harm or suicide later in life.

Chapter Eleven

A NECESSITY FOR TEENAGERS TO AVOID BEING BULLIED

With a clear understanding of teenage bullying, it is also essential to understand the necessity for teenagers to avoid bullying. If by this time, you are still reading this book, you must have learned a lot about bullying. What matters at this point is that you know the reasons to avoid being bullied or becoming a part of it. Protecting teenagers from being bullied is also important because it can leave long term effects on them. Bullying among children will often relate to the development of negative emotions which can cause negative thinking.

People who are bullied at a young age face difficulties in retrieving confidence. It can make them anxious and insecure about themselves. Teenagers should focus on staying connected with friends and seeking support when needed. Children who are exposed to bullying are perceived as a little different from their peers such as being disabled, under/overweight, skin color, race/religion, and social status/clothing.

You should avoid being bullied because it can make teenagers depressed which is an important driver of suicidal thoughts. Depression and anxiety become friends with teenagers when they fail to find supportive friends. For teenagers, it is vital to know that bullying can cause health-related problems. To avoid bullying at school, this is what you should be doing:

- Appear confident in front of your bully.
- Be Assertive and clear so that your bully can know you are NOT weak.
- Build self-esteem because it is the core component that works for bullying prevention.
- Nurture interactions and friendships because bullies will always look for people who are isolated.
- Put the blame of bullying where it

belongs: **To the bully.**

Maintain eye contact with the person who is trying to bully you. Remember, you don't have anything to hide or be afraid of.

Make Early Recovery Possible for Victims

Recovering from bullying effects is as tricky and challenging as recovering from surgery. You feel exposed, vulnerable, broken, and hurt. However, this does not matter at all. What matter is when you start recovering! The moment you allow yourself to recover is when all your pain starts vanishing. It is never you who is at fault. The recovering procedure can become easy if you show courage and confidence. For a victim, early recovery can be made possible by providing them space, assurance, and support. The only way you can initiate the healing process is to **'Let Go of Victim Thinking'**.

The feeling of injustice can creep you out and eat your sense of reasoning all at once. However, you should know when to let go of it. You can initiate the healing process as soon as you let go of the thoughts that tell you about being a victim. The feeling of injustice can help you start interactions that are effective in maintaining the mindsets of children. The prevention of victim-thinking can help you avoid getting emotionally pulled into some trap. Teenagers viewing the world with judgment glasses will find it difficult to maintain a stable mindset.

It will surely begin when you leave judgment because it can help children becoming emphatic and understanding. Healing for bullying victims should be based on the fact that they are not what they say or call them. Instead, after being subjected to bullying, they can't form an opinion about themselves. Being the victim of bullying lets you remember some cruel episodes of mistreating throughout your life. But it does not mean that you can't recover from the state. First, it is important to focus on having a sense of belongingness among people. It is further related to the essential needs of human beings.

ENCOURAGING GOOD BEHAVIOR IN TEENAGERS

At a very initial stage, bullying can be stopped by encouraging good behavior in teenagers. The sense of responsibility among teenagers can help them become better citizens. Bullying is a social subject because it is growing increasingly common across the globe. It is simple to understand sometimes when a bully tries getting a victim under his evilness. However, in some cases, bullying can become complicated because it is pervasive, especially in terms of addressing bullying and alleviating it.

Teenagers need to be reminded about their belongingness and acceptance for initiating and accelerating the healing problem.

Let Them Know, You care!

The sense of belongings can help teenagers in discussing and forming relationships. Shutting down during a conflict, falling in perpetual isolation and trust issues become the evidence of bullying effects. Being a teenager, you should know that you will have many opportunities in life. With these opportunities, you can ensure self-acceptance and confidence. For parents and guardians, it is important to encourage children to behave ethically even with strangers.

Teachers, parents, and guardians can collectively work for cultivating good behavior among children. Educating teenagers about bullying and abuse is important because it will help them in knowing the limits that no one should cross.

The education and awareness about bullying will enable children in detecting bullying at its initial stages. Being treated right! This is what everyone should know about. Teachers and parents are responsible for informing children about the way they should be treated.

Psychological development of children is related to their awareness and acknowledgment about the do's and don'ts of bullying. This education will also help teenagers in avoiding bullying at school. What these children need to hear is:

- No one can treat you badly on the basis of your skin color.

- Your grades do not define you as a person so don't let anyone else to that to you.

- Your social status, clothes, and choices have nothing to do with anyone, so don't let a bully tell you anything about it.

- Your disability is actually you different-ability (Never forget that).

- Your race/religion and cultural background have nothing to do with your social acceptance.

- No one can share your videos, media files, photos, and other content without your permission.

- No one can blackmail you into doing anything that you don't want to do.

- They have no right to tell you who you are and how you are.

WHO NEEDS TO ACT AND WHO IS ACTING FOR ITS PREVENTION?

After looking at bullying and its effects, we need to explore the options that one can adopt for its prevention. Before proceeding in this direction, it is important for the reader to know 'Who Needs to Act' for preventing bullying. Teenage bullying often takes place in school. In fact, it will not be wrong to say that most of the teenage jealousies and bullying arise from school fights. Since schools are the central hub where bullying starts, it is essential for educational representatives to accelerate their actions toward preventing school bullying. Educational authorities are obliged to keep a close check on the behavior of children in school.

They should monitor the ways in which teenage students handle conflicts and treat each other. Considering the increasing awareness among people about bullying, several anti-bullying campaigns are formed that are working in Canada, the UK, and the USA. These campaigns can help people in fighting teenage bullying at its core. In most regions of the United States, Canada, and the United Kingdom, anti-bullying laws are imposed with the end goal of eliminating this problem at its root.

However, at the individual level, teachers and parents can play an active role in detecting bullying and helping teenagers. Teachers and parents are also obliged to focus on improving personality and character development of children. They should be aware of the consequences attached to bullying. In simple words, the following are the strategies that teachers should be adopting for reducing bullying cases among teenagers. Teachers should educate children about the importance of kindness and empathy.

They should discourage them from name-calling and trolling during, before, and after the class. During school premises, teachers should make sure that children are on their best behaviors. Allow children to know each other through offering opportunities. Know of any backbencher gang trolling children during lectures? Break them and divide them, so that children can form connections with everyone. Likewise, teachers can also follow these practices for eliminating bullying among children:

- Refer to and maintain school rules and regulations

- Support the bullied child and give them confidence

- Offer support and guidance for bystanders

- Encourage children to follow ethics and morals

- Make sure to notify colleagues and parents about the incidents

- Avoid confusing bullying as a random conflict between teenagers

- Avoid group treatment for bullies

As far as parents are concerned, as soon as they

detect any kind of bullying symptom in their child's behavior, they should act and call the school. Parents should push schools to take immediate action against bullying because it is essential for a child's mental health. Parents are also encouraged to develop a strong bond with their children so that they can share their problems with them. Apart from these actions, parents should be doing these to eliminate bullying:

- Tell your child repeatedly that they have got your back no matter what
- Ask them to share their daily routine and school stuff
- Let them be comfortable with you always so that they will at least have someone trustable
- Let them know about your concerns and inform them about the ways they can deal with it
- Maintain eye contact and a friendly relationship with them
- Know your child's friend

- Teach them how to stand up against peer pressure

- Teach your children to be compassionate

Websites and Help Centers Where Teenagers Can Report

Several help centers are working against teenage bullying. Before looking at these websites and help centers, it is important to know are these accessible to children or not? Teachers and guardians are responsible for providing the necessary basic information about using help centers against bullying. Children can only take action against bullying if they are aware of their rights.

They should know what bullying is, and how another bunch of students is practicing it against you. The rise in the knowledge and awareness of people about bullying becoming a social problem has pushed them to develop safe places for teenagers. Before going to these websites and help centers, this is what children should try:

- Involve an Adult

- Tell your Teacher

- Let Your Parents Know Everything

Coming back to the websites and help centers, these are campaigns that are working against bullying in the Western world:

- Act against Bullying
- BeatBullying
- Bystander Revolution
- Ditch the Label
- Kidscape
- Jer's Vision

Like these, many other websites are there that are available for children, so that they can deal better with bullying. Let these websites, teachers, and parents help you! Teenage bullying should not be treated lightly. It is important to encourage children to speak out and make better individual choices. Seeking help is important because it can help us in avoiding problems altogether. Every teenager deserves a bullying free life!

CONCRETE ACTIONS/TIPS TO AVOID PHYSICAL, VERBAL, SOCIAL, PSYCHOLOGICAL AND CYBER BULLYING

Bullying is dangerous for physical as well as emotional health of children. There are some concrete actions or tips that people can take to avoid Physical, Verbal, Social, Psychological and Cyber Bullying. These concrete actions are for students, parents, and teachers.

FOR STUDENTS:

- To avoid being bullied in schools, students must stop living in fear.

- They can easily avoid bullying by being vocal about it.

- Students should immediately inform an elder be it a parent or teacher about bullying encounter.

- Students should also take some self-defense classes so that they can learn not only to defend themselves, but also acquire confidence that they will need in order to stand up to bullies.

FOR TEACHERS

- Teachers can play a major role in preventing bullying incidents at school through being knowledgeable and observant.

- Teachers and administrators in school need to be aware of the areas which has become bullying grounds on the premises of the school.

- Teachers should set positive expectations about the behavior of children and adults.

- Effective and strict disciplinary actions should be taken against the students involved in bullying.

- To avoid it at its core, teachers should clearly communicate the consequences of bullying for children.

PARENTS

- Parents can help their children in avoiding bullying.
- For this reason, parents need to teach their children confidence and self-believe.

- Parents should encourage children to form strong bonds with others.
- Inform them about the negative impacts that bullying can leave on a person and inform them not to bully anyone, not even in response.
- Parents should also make sure to involve teachers and bully after seeing an inappropriate behavior taking place in school premises.

Chapter Twelve

WHAT TO DO WHEN YOU SPOT A BULLY?

Ever wondered what you should be doing with this uninvited guest who seems to be comfortable in roasting you or someone else in front of the whole school during lunch break? The least you can do at this point is refusing to join them. Bullies encourage other students to participate in bullying. It is vital to know what you should do when you spot a bully. Spotting a bully is easy and common because these types of people can be seen anywhere.

Now that you know the consequences, teenagers must stay away from such people. Apparently, the majority of us have seen someone being bullied at some point. For every viewer, it is easy to just stand and witness the situation or even to laugh at it. However, doing what needs to be done to stop bullying is what only a courageous person can do. As said, "**You can't be against bullying without actually doing something about it.**" So, here is what you should be doing when you spot a bully next time:

DON'T JOIN OR WATCH

Being a teenager, you should never participate in such acts. Participating in bullying can cause severe reputational damage for you. And let's not forget, bullying is misconduct which has severe punishments attached to it. So, be smart, and try to stay away from people who have a bad reputation or are involved in bullying of any kind. Avoidance is the ultimate cure for many problems.

STOP RUMORS

It is the right of every child to live a bullying-free life. Harassment and bullying can cause severe challenges for victims. The only thing, bullies are good at is spreading rumors; false, fake, and dirty rumors. When you spot a rumor, try to stop it. The only way to stop it is by avoiding repeating it. Sometimes, bullies try to spread rumors that can damage victims' reputation in school. You need to stop repeating those rumors so that you are not participating in this evil act.

STAY FIRM AND OFFER SUPPORT

You are being nice when you are not bullying people. But do you know? You are being kind when you stand up against the bully! If you see someone being bullied, you need to offer support. The victim will badly need your support because humiliation can affect a teenager's self-esteem. So, when you spot a bully, you need to be friendly and concerned. The show of care can do wonders for the victim. You can inspire change by just showing up for someone who needs help. Be the helping hand for them.

TELL AN ADULT

After witnessing bullying, the first thing you should do is to tell an adult. Involving an adult will help in saving the victim and avoiding the issue. It is important for the person to feel comfortable in telling or involving an adult.

SPARE NO DETAILS

Everyone has their own bullying story, whether as a victim or as a witness. And let's be real, peeling the curtain off on your own bullying story is challenging for both the victim and bystander. In both cases, details play a significant role in stopping it at its source. While involving an adult, you need to be very clear. It is important to tell each and everything to the adult or the person getting involved so that they can have a better understanding of the seriousness of the situation. Sparing a few details can put you in trouble later.

SEEK SUPPORT

Spotting a bully when you are the victim will require you to seek help. Try telling it to your friends and teachers, so that you can get a better solution to this problem. Seeking support will scare away your bully—understand that it can be a huge turning point for you. It will show them that you are strong. Finding support can also help in eliminating bullying instantly because most children try you when they believe you are alone and too afraid to go complaining.

ENCOURAGE REPORTING BULLYING

For a teenager, it is important to stand up to all forms of bullying. However, it is even more important for a bystander to stand with you. You have to become that bystander who is courageous enough to stand with the victim. If you are not the victim, you are supposed to encourage the person to report bullying.

Most of the times, bullies get their way because victims do not speak. If you have witnessed bullying, you need to encourage the victim to speak up, so that concerned bodies can act out against bullying. The encouragement can help them in sharing the situation with a trustworthy individual.

LISTEN WITHOUT JUDGEMENT

The victims are sensitive because they have faced public humiliation and insult. It is important to return them their confidence. What can you do? Listen to them without judging them. Listening will do wonders for their self-esteem. The victims are in their state due to their powerlessness. Their inability to share and tell others will make them vulnerable and easy targets for the bullies. As a teenager, you should focus on extending your support for the victims.

EDUCATE

It is high time for people to focus on stopping bullying because it can turn out to be a threat to a teenager's life. The most important measure that one can take when a bully is spotted is educating. It is important for the bystanders to group up and educate the bully. Another notable example is related to the kind of bullying in which the victim is bullied due to different religious beliefs and race. We focus a lot on our differences, and that is cultivating hate among people. Against such bullying, you can try teaching bullies as well as bystanders, so that they can readily accept diverse people. Talking about multiculturalism and diversity can also eliminate the chances of bullying. If you are capable enough, try teaching people about the race or religion of the victim, so that they can empathize with the victims.

Chapter Thirteen

BULLYING AND SUICIDE - DOES IT MAKE SENSE?

Bullying often results in suicide attempted by the victims because it is an unpleasant and challenging aspect of an adolescent's life. Statistically speaking, every year, thousands of suicide cases are reported. These cases often bring a discussion about the connection between bullying and depression among children. Ending life is the nastiest solution available for children because they are too shy and afraid to speak up. Bullying works like a slow poison that can encourage teenagers to take their life.

At first, it encourages teenagers to isolate themselves. As a result, they are left alone and helpless which can further trigger their insecurities. Bullying and suicide have become increasingly common in the Western world. As per the results presented by Stop Bullying Campaign, bullying alone cannot push children to attempt suicide; instead, bullying is linked with depression, stress, trauma, and anxiety which can collectively push teenagers to take this step and end their life.

The suicide risk among teenagers is increasing day by day because they lack social, emotional, and physical support available for them. Primarily, every child has encountered name-calling and rumor-spreading at some point. It is important for concerned bodies to undertake suitable measures for assessing a child's mental health and stability. Monitoring child behavior can help in detecting bullying causes and issues. Encouraging children to speak up about bullying can be useful since it can eliminate the chances or risk of attempting suicide.

CYBERBULLYING

You can see so much bullying and so much negativity on social media. In fact, bullying happens at all ages and levels. The shift in global trends offered a new space for bullies to channelize their frustration and low-self-esteem issues via cyberbullying. Due to this kind of bullying, people often find that social media brings vulnerability to their existence. Cyberbullying is the newest trend in the social world because it works as an '**Online form of harassment'** for teenagers. The proliferation of smartphone along with the rise of social media has transformed how, when, and where bullying takes place.

Cyberbullying accounts for 40% of total bullying cases in this era. It is a widely spreading issue across the globe. Many young girls have fallen victim to this threat. It is risky because it can happen at any time of the day and at any place. With the rise in technology across the globe, texting, tweeting, and digital sharing have become a central way teens form and maintain relationships in this era. The increased level of connectivity has brought new risks for teenagers such as the exchange of explicit messages, potentially troubling and nonconsensual exchange of data and information. Harassment and bullying affect teenagers in many ways. Teenage girls are more targeted in cyberbullying because they are likely to face trolling, and exchange of explicit, nonconsensual texts.

The exchange of these texts can form rumors

against female victims. In this era, teenagers are addicted to social media. For them, social presence and fan following have become significant concerns. With the rise in cyberbullying issues, it is important to look at the way it works. Teenagers often bully other students by destroying their social image and reputation. They have extensively reported that they witness malicious behavior on social media. In Cyberbullying, the misuse of personal information and pictures has become common. The maintenance of social media trends is becoming important for children who often fall into cyber traps. For teenagers, social existence and fan following are essential. Thereby, they will prefer abusing someone online, instead of doing it in person. When it comes to cyberbullying, girls are not only likelier to become a victim than boys are, but they are also more at risk of forming emotional problems and instabilities after being bullied. Statistics presented by PEW Research center suggested that around 60% of girls have experienced harassment at least one in every six times they are online.

This bullying is not just limited to name-calling

and spreading rumors, but it includes the exchange of pictures, pornography/adult content, and intimidating messages. Girls are likelier to be in the list of recipients of explicit and unethical messages that they did not ask for. We can't blame cellphones as the only source of cyberbullying because along with the access to smartphone and tablets, internet-related harassments have also become a matter of concern. Girls receiving inappropriate images online from anonymous accounts tells a lot about cyberbullying.

GROWING UP ONLINE – HOW DO THEY BULLY YOU?

Growing up online lets you see different types of bullies. Online and offline bullying are equally destructive. There is a list of social media sites that teenagers use to stay connected and updated. Being a social animal is what every teenager wants these days. In the wake of becoming popular, most teenagers fall in the trap of cyberbullying. Now that you understand cyberbullying, do you know the types of online bullying you meet? Well, be clear that cyberbullying is not just limited to **'receiving**

inexplicit anonymous messages and texts'.

Cyberbullying is 'Exclusion': it happens when bullies deliberately exclude you from online groups without any reason. It is when they make you feel left out and ignored. They deliberately want you to feel excluded because this can hurt you. Another type of cyberbullying is 'Gossiping' which happens when they post about you, talk about you, discuss you, and leave no stone unturned to damage your reputation both online and offline. Look for the people who unnecessarily drag you in the conversations that can make you uncomfortable and uneasy.

You must have heard about stalking when looking up someone's profile online. But have you ever heard about cyberstalking? How does it happen? And what are the consequences? Well, cyberstalking is an important type of cyberbullying because it is about posting or sending unwanted messages and silently following victims. Let's say, crush stalking is cute but it can sometimes cause problems for you! Keeping track of a person's online activities that have no concern with you makes you a cyber-stalker. Cyberstalking sometimes may or may not include threats for the victim. In any way, cyberstalking is unethical, and teenagers should be aware of it.

Cyber-stalkers can manipulate people around you because they are the first ones gossiping about you. Apart from cyber-stalkers, you meet numerous kinds of harassers online. Harassment is when someone is posting stuff about you online which is not just offensive, but false too in most cases. Harassers send you dirty or insulting messages because they want to embarrass you about something you never did. It can further lead towards outing and trickery. Basically, tricking someone online is unethical and unpleasant, but harassers do it all the time, and they trick you into revealing secrets which they can share later and embarrass you. Cyber-threats are real: as real as the internet itself! One in every five teenagers receives threat messages online. For teenagers, cyber-threats are prevalent because of the proliferation of the internet and social media usage have made them easy targets. The threats are often comprised of fake details that they can use for hurting others. It occurs when they share your fake profiles online. Cyberbullying is not limited to boys. Teenage girls are vulnerable too because they are easily targeted. For teenage girls, cyberbullying becomes a reason for stress.

For every teenager, it is important to understand the consequences of cyberstalking and trolling. Cyberstalking is the form of online harassment that young girls face. It is different from trolling where people tend to provoke others intentionally or unintentionally. It is a nightmare for many young girls. Statistically speaking, around 23% of young people face cyberbullying online say that they were tricked and sexually harassed online.

HARMFUL EFFECTS OF CYBERBULLYING

Cyberbullying is not inevitable, but its effects are! A bully behind a keyboard is still a bully. Cyberbullying can cause severe psychological and emotional effects on teenagers. We can avoid its consequences by addressing it as early as possible. It can make victims violent, abusive, and confused. In many instances in the United States, teenagers admitted to becoming violent and angry. The anger and vengeance can affect academic as well as the social performance of victims. The most important effect of cyberbullying is related to depression. Being in depression can make you vulnerable because it often leads to suicide.

Depression is real and can make people stop living. Every teenager deserves a peaceful and happy life. Depression is undoubtedly becoming the leading cause of teenage death. Cyberbullying is creepy because it has the tendency to go unnoticed for a while. The late detection of cyberbullying makes it even scarier for teenagers. It is bad for a teenager's mental as well as physical health because it can trigger anxiety among children. It is important to know the consequences of bullying on personal development.

Cyberbullying can lead to self-harm and suicidal thoughts. The endpoint of these thoughts is an attempted suicide. Many children reflect unstable emotional status post bullying in the form of eating and sleeping disorders. Teenagers show disinterest in everything they do or wherever they go if they face bullying. Another vital sign depicting cyberbullying for a teenager can be observed in their hesitation in going online or even talking about social media. Beware of the changes in the behavior of teenagers around you!

Chapter Fourteen

DEALING WITH CYBERBULLYING

If you are a parent, here are some reminders that you have to give your kids in order to deal with cyberbullying. If they find themselves in a situation wherein, they are targeted by the cyberbullies, remind them that it is not their obligation to respond to the posts or messages thrown at them. No matter how hurtful the accusations maybe or no matter how made up or untrue their posts are, remind them not to react. Reacting or posting a response will only "feed the troll." That is exactly what they want, to get the potential victim's attention. Eventually, they will stop when they see that the potential victim is non-responsive. They do not get any satisfaction from targets that do not react.

In addition, and more importantly, you need to point out to your child that it is wrong to seek vengeance or to take any revenge. This is the origin of role reversals wherein former victims become the tormentors. This will only make things a lot worse that they were before. Point out the fact that cyberbullies have a lot more reasons to be anxious.

So, what's the appropriate response to cyberbullying, then? Here are some of the tried and tested ways:

1) Take screen shots and properly document all the evidence of cyberbullying. If they are in the form of SMS, keep them intact in the phone's inbox. Consult other adults, preferably educators or law enforcers to know what the next action would be. Tell your child that it is best to let an adult know. Tell him that he should not bear the pain alone.

2) If the cyberbullying already involves sexual predation, call the police. Again, document all evidence. Such online sexual predation can be properly dealt with by the full force of the law.

3) Do not put down the defense. Again, cyberbullying is something that can go on

for a long period of time. It does not happen in one go. So, if such an illegal act goes on for a period of time, then your defense should last that long too. Do not stop guarding your child from cyberbullies. Never get tired of reporting the incidents until the cyberbully is punished.

4) Tell the victim not to attempt establishing a communication between him and the cyberbully. Additional lines of defense should also be done – block the e-mail addresses used, report the mobile phone number, and ban the social media contact. It would also be wise to report the user which persistently cyberbullies the kid.

Here are some things that you should tell a victim:

- It is not his fault, so there is no point blaming him for what happened. The cyberbully usually chooses his target arbitrarily. Never think that the cyberbully has a point. Usually, they do not tell the truth.

- You need to see the incident of

cyberbullying from a different point of view. Look at the cyberbully with pity because he does not have a life. He might have become what he is because he is frustrated and because he is sad. Never feel bad about yourself. Feel bad about the cyberbully.

- Never punish yourself because of the cyberbullying. Wallowing on the cyberbullying incident won't help. Do not make a big deal out of it. It will not even help if the victim will read the message again and again. Encourage the victim to think of happy thoughts and put his focus on the positive events in his life. Tell the victim that he is a blessed and wonderful person no matter what other people say.

- Do not hesitate to ask help from any adult. When your child encounters a cyberbully, make him promise that he will tell you right away. If the parent is not within reach, then tell him that he should report any cyberbullying incident to a counselor, a teacher, a police, or any adult whom he trusts.

- Learn to positively react to stress. You need to find a way to lessen the stress. Teach your child how to meditate, to exercise, to do self-affirmation, and to be optimistic. By doing any of these, your child will soon get over the negative effects of cyberbullying.

- Do the things that you are passionate about. The more enjoyable it is, the better. For as long as it can help the victim forget, it will definitely work. It can be anything – sports activities, socialization with the people you love, doing your interests, playing games – for as long as it can help the victim cope from the effects of cyberbullying.

Chapter Fifteen

OTHER THINGS THAT SHOULD BE REMEMBERED ABOUT CYBERBULLYING

Any type of bullying – be it the traditional or the cyber version – can lead to harm, anger, helplessness, and isolation. But did you know that these are also the main causes of bullying? Minors who have experienced too much hurt, anger, helplessness, and isolation are the most likely candidates to become a cyberbully. Ultimately, victims fall into the trap of anxiety, low level of self-esteem, and depression. The following are some reasons on why cyberbullying is more difficult to deal with:

- First and foremost, cyberbullying is more painful and usually, the suspect is faceless and nameless. Face-to-face bullies have more vulnerability compared to a cyberbully.

- Cyberbullying is an event that can occur at any time. It is also not location specific. Cyberbullied kids can be attacked inside their own rooms. Though there are adults around, they can be subjected to hurtful attacks. Though the attacks will never leave any physical mark, cyberbullying victims are literally scarred forever.

- Quite conveniently for cyberbullies, they can do the deed without even having to hand in their identity. Based on the latest research, majority of online bullies are doing their attacks using anonymous accounts. This is painful for the bullied kid because he cannot even see who his attacker is. The threat is too real yet they cannot see where the shots are being fired from. Anonymity, in the online context, means that it is difficult to catch a bully and punish him for what he does. Often times, they do not hold any responsibility over the results of their actions and they tend to go too far in hurting their prospective victims.

- Cyberbullying has an audience that is way larger than you think. Usually, a kid bullied over Facebook is humiliated in front of his friends, his friends' friends, and it can be forwarded to other people. This kind of bullying reaches really far.

While cyberbullying can really be hurtful, it does not mean that there is nothing that you can do. In this chapter, we will do a recap on how to effectively react to cyberbullying in order to put it to stop:

- The cyberbully should be ignored. Eventually, an ignored bully would stop his negative deeds. Reacting to the bully feeds his imagination and encourages him to continue. A reaction is a cyberbully's come on.

- The cyberbully's activities should be recorded and documented fully. Take a screen cap of everything and do not forget to keep a record in print. It is easier to study your options if you have a hard copy documentation of all bits of evidence.

- The victim should be encouraged to reach out to the people whom he should trust.

There are rules that can protect the bully, but he should seek out some help first.

Finally, you need to remember what you have to avoid when dealing with the bullies:

- Never stoop down to the level of the bully. Do not follow his ways. Tell your child that the bully is a law breaker; copying his ways will make him a criminal, too.

- Never forward the bully's message to your friends and to other people your age. Reserve the "sharing" with the trustworthy adults only who knows what to do. Forwarding the bully's message will only create a bigger problem.

- Never validate the bully's action by believing what he is doing. No one has given the bully the right to tell anything hurtful to you. It is wrong to take the bully seriously. Who should believe a faceless and heartless online entity who can't even talk to you face to face?

This compilation is a work in progress. As technology becomes more modern, cyberbullying also evolves. The battle is far from over, but you can always win over the bully.

Chapter Sixteen

BENEFITS OF BULLYING

While it may seem contrary to rational belief, some studies suggest that being bullied can also promote positive growth in those being bullied. While it certainly won't seem that way to start, being bullied as a child can actually help those who are bullied see positive emotional and social development from the experiences.

IT IS NOT ALL BAD

In fact, while it seems that roughly 40 percent of all of those in middle and high school suffered from some type of bullying, a majority of those ultimately end up doing quite fine in life, with some 40 percent of the original 40 percent even going on to do significantly better than the general average. The studies go on to suggest that the over exaggeration of those who do find themselves bullied to the extreme comes from the fact that the smallest percentage of those under the age of 18 who are bullied often create extreme responses instead of shrugging it off as most seem to do. Teens who get revenge in horrific ways or those who take their misery out on themselves are simply an extremely vocal minority.

In fact, a recent study found that, perhaps unsurprisingly, those who stood up to their bullies when pressed, found it less difficult to stand up for themselves when the need arises later on in life. The results of standing up for themselves also becomes more immediately apparent as those who stood up to their bullies tended to be more mature and have a more concrete grasp of the benefits of conflict resolution. Furthermore, it gives them a more well-rounded view of the world as they learn that not everyone is always going to like them despite what may well be their best efforts to influence an outcome to the contrary.

Those who are bullied have an outlet for negative thoughts and emotions

Another surprising finding seems to be that students who reciprocate hostile feelings, and possibly actions, when it comes to dealing with bullies, actually tend to score higher on things like social competence when tested against their peers. When presented with a bully, students have the opportunity to either turn the other cheek, which can ultimately be fruitless, ignore the issue which rarely makes it go away, or they can engage which can create significant social gains when done in front of a group.

This is likely due to the fact that the human brain enjoys patterns, often even going so far as to create them where none previously existed, when applied to relationships, this love of patterns manifests itself in the natural predilection to enjoy symmetry in existing relationships. This means that children will naturally like those who also appear to like them while the reverse is also true. To take it a step further, children them typically project traits they admire and want to embody onto those they like and the traits they hate about themselves onto those they dislike.

As such, those who have an antagonist relationship in their lives more easily learn what type of behavior is morally repulsive and have a mirror by which their negative traits can be reflected in the most effective way possible.

Those who experience a tyrannical bully when they are young, have a much more difficult time lording their power over others in the future.

Having a common enemy teaches valuable lessons

Regardless of all other factors, when a group of individuals has an external threat to unite them, they will work together more effectively, remaining happier and more willing to sacrifice personal happiness for the good of the group for longer periods of time. A bully can be this external threat to a group of individuals and as long as the threat is at large, they will find that all other group related squabbles fall by the wayside. The bonds of those who are standing up to the external threat will last far beyond the event in question.

For children, being bullied provides them with the opportunity to solve a real world problem that is at once big enough that solving it will represent a milestone between childhood and the burgeoning world of adult problems and responsibilities. At the same time, the problem that presents itself is still firmly rooted in the rules of childhood, which makes it the perfect symbolic step towards maturation that all children must eventually come to terms with.

In addition, allowing the antagonistic relationship between bully and victim to form naturally as the result of betrayal can provide lifelong benefits, though the initial shock will no doubt be substaintial. The understanding that people are not always what they seem is a valuable lesson to learn and those who learn it at an early age are less likely to be taken advantage of at an older age when the repercussion of such a betrayal are likely to be much more serious than a few hurt feelings.

Coming into contact with this sort of experience will also allow children to determine what sort of person they would like to be in turn because they have a broader view of the possible spectrum of human behavior. Children learn how to be the adults they become by mimicking the behavior of the adults they see around them but also by having negative experiences that show them how not to act in future situations. In fact, the earlier the negative behavior is experienced the more likely that the child in question pivots more dramatically in the opposite direction.

Response is important

Ultimately, it appears as though the response to

the bullying, both from the bullied and the bullied child's parents goes a long way to determining how the child will respond to the bullying. This means it is important to never treat the childas if they were the victim of something serious while at the same time not downplaying the issue to the point that the child feels as though their feelings regarding the issue are not valid. It is important to make the child feel as though their feelings about the situation are worthwhile while still providing a positive framework where they can work through the issue by themselves.

Chapter Seventeen

THE BULLYING EPIDEMIC

"Bullying is never fun, it's a cruel and terrible thing to do to someone. If you are being bullied, it is not your fault. No one deserves to be bullied, ever." - Raini Rodriguez

With the story of Ryan Patrick Halligan, we see just how horrible bullying really is. And it's just one of the millions of stories of how people, both children and adults, are bullied and the damage it wreaks on their lives. But essentially, what really is bullying? Is picking on people enough to be considered bullying?

A bullying behavior is one that's aggressive and thrives on an imbalance of power and repetition. Bullies normally have significantly greater "power" – such as popularity, access to confidential information and physical strength – than the ones being bullied and use such power to harm or control others who are deemed to be less powerful. Such power imbalance however, doesn't have to remain constant and there are instances that it changes or shifts over time, even with the same cast of characters. Bullies also do this more than once or at the very least, has a very high potential and capability to do it over and over should they desire to do so. Intentionally excluding someone from a group, verbally or physically attacking people, spreading malicious rumors and threatening are some of the ways bullying is done on the weaker party or parties.

There are 3 general ways people bully other people: verbal, social and physical. Verbal bullying is writing to or saying mean things about another person, which includes among others threats, taunts, inappropriate sexual comments, calling of name and teasing.

Social bullying on the other hand, involves harming others' relationships or reputation – also called relational or reputational bullying. Social bullying may take the forms of publicly embarrassing another person, disseminating malicious stuff about others, telling others to ignore or discriminate against someone in particular and intentionally leaving someone out of a group.

Physical bullying is when the bully hurts another person's possessions or body by way of destroying or grabbing someone else's stuff, gesturing rudely with the hands, pushing/tripping, hitting, kicking, spitting and punching, among others.

Bullying can basically happen anytime – during or after school hours, during or after working hours and even during or after any social gathering. While most bullying incidents are reported at school and work, significant percentages of it are now happening – and continue to increase – over the Internet, in the streets or in the playgrounds.

According to the Center for Disease Control and Prevention's 2013 youth risk behavior surveillance system, 20% of grades 9-12 students all over the United States experienced bullying. In a similar report by the National Center for Education Statistics and Bureau of Justice statistics, about 28% of grades 6-12 students also experienced bullying. And these are just the reported cases, what more of the unreported ones?

Conclusion

If you're not being physically threatened or blackmailed, among others, you can opt to resolve it on your own first. The following are tips for dealing with verbal bullying by yourself:

Ignoring Your Bully

As much as possible, ignore the person bullying you. This is most especially helpful and wise especially if the bullying is a once-in-a-blue-moon kind. In many situations, bullies are merely trying to elicit a reaction from you and if you don't give them that satisfaction, they may just get tired and move on.

One way to ignore the bully is to avoid him or her. When you see that person approaching you, just walk away to avoid any confrontation. Just make sure that your body language when walking away is that of a confident one and not of fear and trembling because otherwise, he or she just might hound you.

Another good way of ignoring your bully is by concentrating on something else that you're excited about, like your next out of town trip or that car you've been planning to buy in the next few weeks. If you think about something that's more significant, you can divert your attention away from the bully and be able to ignore him or her. Speaking of distractions, you can also repeat a good statement or mantra inside your head or build an imaginary wall around you that can just bounce off any verbal tirades from the bully.

You want a fun way to ignore your bully? Picture him or her in the most outrageously funny and humiliating costume. That should be enough to help you make light of what he or she's trying to do to you. An example of this would be to imagine him or her wearing only an adult-sized diaper and a gigantic feeding bottle – a literal crybaby.

Keeping a positive attitude or mindset is another good way to ignore your verbal bully. While it may be hard to do so when someone continuously tries to bombard you with verbal negativity, it isn't impossible. Just bring to mind your good qualities that will totally trump the verbal bully's tirades against you. It'll also help you to bring to mind the reasons for bullying enumerated in Chapter 3 – this should help you feel pity for the bully instead of fear or contempt.

Being around people who genuinely care for you and who are also positive can help you be confident enough in yourself to simply ignore your verbal bully's tirades. It'll help the insults simply slide off your back. It'll rob the bully of his or her power to affect you and your self-esteem. When you become more confident and at peace with who you are, verbal bullies won't see you as the weakling they think you are. As such, they'll probably just move on to the next victim knowing it's a losing proposition to continue verbally bullying you. Who knows, it might affect him more than you!

Standing Up to Your Bully

There comes a time when you ignoring your bully simply won't cut it, especially if he or she is already beyond logic and reason. It may already require that you stand up to him or her. Here are a couple of ways you can do so:

-It all begins from inside. To effectively stand up to your bully, you must first be convinced that you have what it takes to do so. To this effect, it will be very helpful to use positive self-talk to build up your self-esteem. Tell yourself that you don't deserve this and the bully has no right to put you down. It will also help you that you are loved and accepted by your family and friends and you don't deserve to be treated that way.

-When you're that secure with yourself, you can afford to shock the living daylights out of your bully by killing him or her with kindness. Being kind and nice to a person who isn't can throw him or her off enough to stop bothering you.

-If kindness doesn't work, simply stand up to the bully and tell that person to get off your back and to leave you. Often times, bullies thrive because the bullied person doesn't retaliate and when the victims finally fight back, they're shocked into their senses and leave them alone.

Consider self-defense options

When it appears as though the person who is bullying you is aiming for a physical confrontation, it is important to always try and mitigate the situation as much as possible using words and calm body language. Especially if there are witnesses around, making it clear that you were not instigating the fight may be important depending the severity of the outcome of the fight in question.

To ensure you are always able to make the right decisions, it is important to understand common signs of aggression in others. This can include but is not limited to an increase in the pitch of the voice, either instances of extreme flushing or paleness, fidgeting or general restlessness, excessive staring without blinking, increased in the rapidness or severity of the breathing, muscle tension, shaking, a clenching of the teeth or jaw or excessive perspiration.

More noticeable signs including, walking in a tight circle, physically attacking objects, stamping feet, rapid changes in focus, a change in the tone of the voice, a dismissal of personal space, swearing, yelling or excessive pointing. These symptoms can be exacerbated by talking to the bully in an extremely familiar tone, by making the issue they are mad about seem trivial, by making assumptions about them, telling them what they did wrong, using complicated jargon or acting patronizing towards them.

Up until the point where you begin to feel physically threatened it is important to try and prevent violence for as long as possible. Consider the following specifics when determining if the time for preventing violence has passed:

Where are the current danger zones and are there any safe zones in the area?

Assess how in control of the current situation you are, are the other people around you listening when you speak?

Are the other people exhibiting signs of aggression?

Taking action

If you do decide to take action, it is important to not hesitate once you have begun to act. You will only have a limited amount of time when surprise is on your side, you will want to use that to your advantage as much as possible. According to the law, any person has the right to use reasonable force in regards to another human being in situations that would result in the prevention of a crime or when taking action to ensure the safety of themselves or others.

In this case, the law only states that force that is used needs to be considered reasonable when compared with the threat that it is used to mitigate as seen by the defender, which in this case would be you. To ensure you come out the victor in the case of a physical altercation keep the following suggestions in mind.

Begin on the defensive

The moment the bully steps towards you with the goal of violence in mind, respond aggressively by pushing at them with your main hand and loudly asserting that they back off. While not terribly aggressive, this move alerts those around you to your plight, makes it clear that you are not the aggressor in the situation for potential legal purposes later and conveys the fact ad that you are not going to be the pushover that the bully likely expected you to be.

Aim for the right parts of the body

Excessive force is rarely considered reasonable except when it comes to extremely dangerous attackers, as such it is important that you make the most of every time you connect with the bully's body to take control of the situation as quickly as possible. In situations where violence is warranted it is likely you or the other person which means it is also no time hold back. Start by aiming for the legs, knees, groin, neck, ears, nose or eyes, avoiding instances of permanent damage wherever possible. Your goal should be to end the fight, not cripple the bully.

When selecting the target to attack, it is important to never close the distance between you and the bully just to attack a more vulnerable section of the body. For example, it is unnecessary to try and punch someone in the nose when you are already in position to kick them in the knee. When aiming for joints it is best to hit them from the side, while the groin and the nose respond most effectively to precise, direct pressure.

When attacking the upper portion of the bully's body it is important to try and always strike in one of three ways, with the outside edge of the hand in what is known as a knife position, a strike with the palm of the hand or a knuckle blow if nothing else seems appropriate. The only time you should strike another person with a tightly closed fist is if you are aiming at a soft part of the body such as the throat.

Make it count

If the situation continues to escalate despite your

best intentions it is perfectly acceptable to go for the eyes using a scratching, poking or gouging motion. The eyes are a great choice if you are trying to escape as attacking this part of the body will cause maximum pain as well as disorientation which can make escape easier. If the bully continues to advance, a swift strike with the palm of your hand pushing upwards against their nose will allow you to put all of your weight behind the attack, nasal bones are weak and the resulting injury produces a lot of blood, a great diversion if a quick getaway is required.

The side of the neck where the jugular and the carotid artery are located is a relatively wide target that, when struck properly, can temporarily stun your bully. To correctly perform this strike you simply hold your hand out straight with the thumb pointed inward and then jab the thumb and the side of your hand into the side of their neck as hard as possible.

When it comes to the lower body the best point of impact is the knee as it is vulnerable from practically all sides and, when enough pressure is applied to it, will cause your bully to crumble to the ground allowing you to escape or to press your advantage to end the fight as quickly as possible. When it comes to attacking the knee, the side or back will cause the bully to fall to the ground, kicking from the front could possibly hobble them for life.

Extreme scenarios

In situations where basic self-defense moves simply do not seem to be working, consider using your head, knees and elbows which will likely inflict the most damage possible, though not without a little, or a lot of pain reciprocated across your body as well. These three parts of your body are the boniest which means they pack the most wallop as well. It is also important to think about the differences in size and athleticism between you and your opponent. If you are the larger of the two, try and use your weight and reach to your advantage; if you are the smaller of the two, make your extra speed count.

Finally, it is important to not discount the value of things like keys or pens as weapons, though you should always think carefully about using them and to only do so when you honestly feel as though your life is in danger. A fistfight might result in an assault charge, bringing a weapon into play could easily escalate much, much, higher. It is important to always stop the fight as soon as the threat has realistically passed and never press an advantage once the bully has conceded the fight otherwise you might now be considered the aggressor.

Depending on the area you are in, the environment can also offer up a bevy of tools to make the fight easier. Consider using garbage to your advantage or even something as simple as throwing sand or dirt into your opponent's eyes. Likewise, take the time to consider the footing where the fight is taking place, a well-placed push at the right place and time could send the bully tumbling, drastically changing the pacing of the fight in your favor.

Made in the USA
Middletown, DE
28 April 2022